CITIES UNDER STRESS

CITIES UNDER STRESS

CAN TODAY'S CITY SYSTEMS BE MADE TO WORK?

BY KATHLYN GAY

1985
FRANKLIN WATTS
AN IMPACT BOOK
NEW YORK • LONDON
TORONTO • SYDNEY

Photographs courtesy of: UPI/Bettmann Archive:
pp. 2, 7, 13, 29, 38, 47, 50; Bay Area Rapid Transit: p. 26;
Baltimore Convention and Visitors Bureau: p. 55;
Michigan Travel Commission: p. 62; Frank Sloan: pp. 65, 76.

Library of Congress Cataloging in Publication Data

Gay, Kathlyn.
Cities under stress.

(An Impact book)
Includes index.
Summary: Describes and analyzes the stresses and
strains on urban systems in the United States and the
decline of living conditions in many of them.
Also suggests some factors that make certain cities
desirable places to live.
1. Cities and towns—United States—Juvenile literature.
2. Municipal government—United States—Juvenile
literature. 3. Quality of life—United States—Juvenile
literature. [1. Cities and towns. 2. Municipal government.
3. Quality of life] I. Title.
HT123.G35   1985   307.7′64′0973   84-21891
ISBN 0-531-04926-4

51819

87-16081

CONTENTS

COLLAPSING NETWORKS

CHAPTER ONE

BRIDGE FALLS; THREE DIE. The newspaper headline announced the tragedy in late June 1983. Along Interstate 95 in Connecticut, a 100-foot (30-m) span of bridge over the Mianus River collapsed. Two tractor-trailers and several cars plunged 70 feet (21 m) into the water. Three people were killed and three others were seriously injured. State authorities said they had no idea what caused the bridge to crumble. But for months before the accident, people living in the area had reported seeing chunks of concrete fall off and hearing strange creaks and other vibration noises from the twenty-five-year-old bridge.

The I-95 bridge is just one of the thousands that are rusting and crumbling. Nearly 45 percent of the nation's 557,516 bridges need repairs or should be replaced. Yet the bridges are just part of the many thousands of miles of federal high-

*Serious questions were asked in June of 1983
when a section of the Mianus Bridge on the
Connecticut Turnpike collapsed, killing three people.*

ways that are falling apart. Some sections of the federal highway system are as bumpy as washboards. Others are hazardous stretches of roadway full of chuckholes and fallen rocks. Some makeshift roads force vehicles to bounce along from one good section of highway to another.

CITY SYSTEMS STRAINED

City roads are falling apart along with interstate highways. Other public facilities such as water and sewer systems are also in trouble. Miami, Florida, for example, has only one clean well for its one million residents. In 1983 tests of other wells in the city showed low levels of toxic chemicals, including arsenic and industrial solvents, in the drinking water.

Miami is not alone in its plight. For nearly a decade cities across the nation have been reporting such chemicals in their drinking water. In New Orleans, to name one, the high cancer rate in the metropolitan area has been linked to the water supply from the Mississippi River, polluted by industrial wastes.

Many cities face serious problems with the systems of tunnels and pipes that carry their water supplies. New York City has just two water tunnels—one nearly forty years old and the other over fifty. Neither has ever been checked. If one tunnel needed repairs or could not function properly, at least a third of the city would be without water. The drought would last not for days or months, but possibly three to five years—until repairs could be made.

Half the sewer systems in the nation are inadequate. Sewage treatment plants need to be enlarged or upgraded. Chicago is just one of many large cities where sewers back up into basements during heavy rains.

Bridges, roadways, and water and sewer systems

are just some of the collapsing networks in cities. Urban experts say the *infrastructure*—a somewhat stuffy term for the various physical systems that keep a city functioning—needs attention in most major cities. Seaports, locks, dams, airports, mass transit systems, public buildings such as prisons, city halls, schools, libraries, and other public facilities are all part of a city's infrastructure. The catchall term also carries with it a list of problems that will cost from $2.5 to $3 *trillion* to overcome, according to "America in Ruins," a recent report presented to Congress.

NEGLECT

One reason public facilities are falling apart can be summed up in a single word: neglect. The nearly 42,955-mile (68,700-km) interstate highway system that connects cities is a good example. Much of the network was built during the late 1950s and through the 1960s. Now some 16,000 to 17,000 miles (25,600 to 27,200 km) of the system have passed their 20-to-25-year life span, and may no longer be safe. By the 1990s about 75 percent of the interstate system will be beyond the safety mark. But little has been done to maintain the highways. At least 12,000 miles (19,200 km) are rated "fair," meaning the roadways may be safe for the top 55-mile-per-hour (88 kph) speed, but they are quickly going to potholes.

Other types of transportation systems have also been neglected because of high costs. Railways across the nation need repairs. Bus and subway systems creak along, but over 100 cities will have to cut mass transit service unless $40 billion in upkeep and replacements is forthcoming.

The list—in billions of dollars—goes on. As the years pass, costs climb. According to one estimate, public works projects that have already been approved by the nation's voters total about $100 billion. But projects have been delayed because taxpayers do not want to vote for higher taxes or bond issues to pay the bills. Delays add about $16 billion a year to the total, since the cost of labor and materials continues to go up.

Yet taxpayers cannot always be blamed for resisting, especially when public works projects have long been subject to fraud and waste. In a number of cities and counties across the nation, government officials have pocketed funds for public works projects that never existed. Others have taken kickbacks—bribe money from companies that have been awarded contracts to sell goods or services to government agencies. The result: higher public works costs. In addition some public works projects are more likely to be funded because they benefit powerful politicians rather than because the projects rank high in terms of need.

Self-serving government officials might also ignore decaying systems, passing on the problems to their successors in office. As one local politician put it: "Who can get excited about leaky pipes? Few people are going to make an issue of something they can't see. Now, if a commuter train is involved in a serious accident or there is some scandal in an overcrowded jailhouse—well, even then voters might want us to take action but not if it's going to cost them an arm and a leg."

TAXPAYER REVOLTS

Many citizen groups have become extremely vocal about the increasingly high costs of government. In recent years taxpayer revolts in several states have added to the problems of funding public works projects. In 1978 California taxpayers led the way, adopting Proposition 13, which represented one type of protest against spiraling property taxes. Proposition 13 re-

2

duced taxes, but at the same time losses in state revenues forced cutbacks in funds for such projects as street and building repairs and flood control. California communities receive a share of the property tax revenue to maintain, improve, or construct public facilities.

According to a 1983 *Los Angeles Times* survey, since 1978 nearly 70 percent of California's cities and counties have been reducing or eliminating services such as street sweeping, groundskeeping, and building upkeep, which have usually been performed by public works departments. Some parts of the state have been hit harder than others. In Los Angeles, for example, the street maintenance crew has been cut almost in half. Road building is nearly at a standstill in some rural areas, although an increase in the gas tax will provide some funds for local street upkeep and road construction.

Many public works officials in the state's major cities worry, however, about raising enough money in taxes and bonds to pay for their crumbling or collapsing public facilities. Citizens simply do not rally around to support infrastructures. "There are no friends of the sewer or society for the preservation of streets," one Oakland official gloomily told the *Times*.

OTHER SYSTEMS UNDER STRESS

"The people are the city," wrote William Shakespeare long ago. Few today would argue the point. People can alter the geography, construct the massive buildings, install the physical systems, and shape the human networks or "people-systems" that make a city work. Some of these people-systems are under as much stress, however, as the infrastructures that seem to be bursting at the seams.

*Cuts in schooling and teachers' pay were protested
in 1978 when Proposition 13 posed a threat.*

Police, firefighters, health workers, educators, and others who provide public services in cities are feeling the strains as cuts are made in city funds. Neighborhood networks in many cities have been undergoing changes. Sometimes thousands of people have been displaced or whole neighborhood communities have been destroyed to make room for highways or "renewal" projects.

The job of governing cities has become more and more complex. Services must be provided for sprawling urban territories as well as densely populated big cities. Since expanding urban areas represent a variety of interests, governments must respond to the needs of the many diverse groups that create stress on political systems.

URBAN AREAS WITHIN A NATIONAL NETWORK

For centuries the world's major cities have been growing rapidly. But in recent years the populations of older cities in the United States (and other industrialized nations) have been declining. Businesses and industries have moved out of established cities, especially in the Northeast and Midwest, to the expanding cities of the Southwest and to more rural areas. As a result these areas have become more urbanized. As suburbs and smaller cities around larger established cities have spread out, their boundaries have met to form what the federal government calls a Standard Metropolitan Statistical Area (SMSA).

Usually a major city is the core of a SMSA. Suburban and urban fringe areas (outer suburbs) are connected to the center city by jobs and other economic activities, and by such cultural opportunities as universities and art centers. Since the 1980 Census some 36

SMSAs have been added to the statistics, making a total of 329 in the nation in 1983.

Some metropolitan areas have become "supercities" as suburbs have expanded and appeared to merge. A southern California supercity includes Los Angeles, Long Beach, San Bernardino, and Riverside, plus all the smaller built-up communities in between. On the East Coast, New York City and its suburbs in northeast New Jersey and southern Connecticut make up the largest supercity in population, with over 17.5 million people.

By the end of 1983 there were twenty-nine supercities with populations of over one million. None of these expansive urban territories has a single overall government or a common legal boundary. But within each supercity the separate urban areas are interdependent.

One of the governmental problems of such a network of urban places is how to coordinate the policies and programs of the individual units so that all can work together. Other questions are raised about public and social services: Who should pay for transit systems that carry people from suburban areas into the city and city residents out to the suburbs? How can a city support recreational, cultural, and educational facilities enjoyed by millions who live both within and outside the city limits? What can be done to insure continual operation of vast networks of utility lines and communicaton systems?

Urban experts must learn how cities can deal with pollution, congestion, noise, and crime. Almost two decades ago the late Robert Kennedy, brother of President John Kennedy, talked about confronting the "urban wilderness," which he called "more formidable" than the wilderness faced by pioneers. Kennedy believed that cities should be places where people "live in dignity and security and harmony, where the great achievements of modern civilization and the ageless pleasures afforded by natural beauty should be available to all."

To reach such a goal, architects, city planners, economists, political scientists, and sociologists (to name a few types of experts) analyze cities as part of a national network. Those who study cities also examine the individual systems—living and physical—that can make urban centers humane and exciting places to live and work. But one of the systems basic to all others is financial. Without the funds to repair, maintain, restore, and improve, many city networks could slowly waste away or collapse.

THE CHAPTER
CITY TWO
CASH
CRUNCH

In his tenth budget message to the Detroit City Council, Mayor Coleman Young explained that the 1983–1984 budget mirrored the "traumatic economic forces which have ravaged this city and the people who live here." The mayor noted that Detroit "has been struggling since 1976 to keep its books balanced." He called this a healthy process "up to a point," since the city had to make sure it was getting the "maximum impact from every dollar spent."

Detroit has, however, been forced to "pare the body of the government . . . beyond fat and into bone," as Young put it. The new budget would "carve away a little more bone." Even though the city had already "reduced the number of fire-fighters by some twenty-five percent," the mayor announced during his budget speech that he would cut more. He also pointed out that the police force had been reduced "to a level not seen since the 1940s," and that the total number of city employees had been reduced "to a level not seen since the 1930s." Yet more cuts would be made.

Slashing budgets has become a familiar exercise for many mayors in cities that are strapped for funds. Because of reduced revenues, thousands of city jobs have been abolished, decreasing services such as those described by Mayor Young. The cash crunch has also forced many cities to shut down job-training programs for the unemployed, and to cut back on a variety of other social services.

WHY THE FISCAL STRAIN?

Plenty of amateur observers as well as professionals in urban affairs are willing to place blame for the financial stress in cities. Some point to poor management of city finances as the cause. Certainly some city administrations have not been willing to make the tough decisions needed to keep costs down, particularly in terms of wage and salary packages. Yet inflation has eroded city budgets as the costs of goods and services have continually gone up. In addition, with the steady migration away from the older urban areas, there are fewer people able to pay for city government. Many of those left in core cities need aid for health, housing, and other social services—placing even more stress on city finances. Federal grants for such services and other types of federal aid have been cut, increasing the burden on city finances.

The recent recession has also had a major impact on cities. When the nation's economy is in trouble, the cities are the first to see the effects. Large manufacturers, like automakers, have to close plants when demands for their products fall off. Usually such plant

A padlock on one of the main gates at
United States Steel's Ohio Works plant tells a
too frequent story of mill and plant closings.

closings occur in central cities, affecting not only jobs but the tax base as well. People who do not have steady incomes cannot pay their property taxes, or buy goods that include sales taxes, or pay for fuel with its added taxes. Businesses are hurt and their share of revenue payments is reduced.

INDUSTRIAL SHIFTS

Changes in the type of industrial development in the nation have also affected the economic health of many older cities. Fewer jobs are available in steel mills and in industries that depend on steel to produce autos, stoves, refrigerators, and similar goods. Heavy manufacturing, for the most part, is located in the Northeast and Midwest (sometimes called the Frostbelt or Snowbelt) where the nation's Industrial Revolution began in the mid-1800s. But the aging industrial plants are losing out to modern facilities built since World War II in other countries. For example, because of lower labor costs and more efficient facilities, steel can be produced more cheaply in the newer plants of Japan and West Germany than in the older mills of Gary, Indiana, and Youngstown, Ohio.

Service industries and light manufacturing (computers and other electronic equipment, pharmaceuticals, and goods based on advanced technology) have become more important to the U.S. economy. Such industries are locating outside major cities since better communication and transportation are now available.

Many manufacturers have also relocated in the Sunbelt. Mild climate, however, is not the main reason for the shift to the South and West. Labor costs are not as high in most Sunbelt cities as they are in the more unionized Frostbelt. Industries are also lured to the Sunbelt by tax incentives. Tax rates for corporations and individuals are lower in the South than in the North. According to *U. S. News and World Report*, local taxes in New York City total over $1,000 per person each year. In Houston, by contrast, total taxes are just over $250; in San Diego, just over $160 per person.

Federal defense contracts have been responsible for the buildup of some Sunbelt cities. Most Defense Department planes and weapons are produced in California, Texas, and Washington, providing higher employment and increased revenues for the cities in those states.

Cities in the South and West have also been helped by increasing energy prices. Oklahoma City, for one, has had a prosperous economy during the early 1980s. Because of higher profits in the oil industry, new jobs have been created and other industries and businesses have expanded. Houston, New Orleans, and San Diego are among other Sunbelt cities that have fared well partly because of oil production and oil-related jobs in industries as diverse as data processors and drilling suppliers.

Despite all the economic development, some cities in the Sunbelt must still deal with financial problems. To accommodate rapidly growing populations, public works have to expand; this can be a strain on city budgets. Although water and sewer systems and similar projects are usually funded, lower taxes have meant fewer social services for citizens. Yet the need for such services in the Sunbelt can be acute. Cities in the Southwest have a larger proportion of poor and lower median incomes than the Frostbelt cities.

WHERE CITIES GET FUNDS

Along with his 1983 budget message, Detroit's Mayor Young submitted charts of revenue sources to the City Council. In any city budget process, the government has to show the income needed to operate for another year. Much of Detroit's income comes from property taxes, city income taxes, and taxes on utilities. The same types of sources support most of the nation's local governments.

Other major revenue sources for cities include taxes collected by the states, such as sales and fuel taxes that are then transferred back to cities. Licenses, fees for various services, and grants from the state and federal governments provide additional income.

Cities can also borrow money to finance public works projects such as sewer systems or fire stations. To borrow money for capital improvements, cities issue bonds that are promises to repay loans with interest. Bond issues, if approved by voters, can help cities improve their capital assets (or public works). In fact, the National League of Cities and the U.S. Conference of Mayors recently surveyed over 800 cities and found that with a "steady but manageable investment over a number of years," cities could fix up public facilities at a "relatively modest" cost, using funds from bond issues.

Although all cities have similar sources of income, each local government has its own revenue structure. While Detroit receives some funds from a city income tax, Chicago's revenue sources include funds from a state income tax. New York City could receive about half its income from state and federal aid, but Houston might receive only 15 to 16 percent in grants from the state and federal governments.

EASING THE CASH CRUNCH

With budget cuts and the struggle to meet expenses, some cities are turning over public works to private companies. Those businesses in turn provide services—trash collection, for example—to residents for a fee. Only those who use the service pay for the costs. In recent years private companies have taken over ambulance services, firefighting, police work, and the operation of libraries, airports, and parks.

Some cities are selling municipal buildings (city halls) to private buyers. Then, in complex legal and tax-benefit packages, city governments have leased back space for their offices. In a number of cities, public buildings such as recreation centers, city garages, and civic centers have been offered for sale. Recently a museum and auditorium in Oakland, California, were sold for $55 million.

One unusual way to ease the cash crunch was undertaken in Portsmouth, New Hampshire. The city created a power plant at the municipal dump. By burning solid waste the plant generates steam that is then sold to a nearby military base. The city earns $2 million a year from the operation.

Many urban experts predict that the blending of public services and private enterprise will continue in the years ahead. In addition there will be an increase in special-purpose authorities and districts. These are independent agencies within a city set up to operate a health care center, park, water system, or other public service. About 29,000 of these units are operating nationwide. They provide the services and collect fees from users.

Critics of the special districts fear that consumers may have to beware. Since independent units are not run by elected officials, there may be few public watchdogs. It could be difficult to determine whether fees charged for services are fair and whether users are getting their money's worth. Critics also question the profit motive when it comes to providing public services that are supposed to protect the lives, health, and property of all citizens, regardless of their ability to pay.

"WISH LISTS"

Along with basic services, cities usually provide some amenities; that is, the extras that add to the quality of urban life. Those amenities may be the first to go with budget cuts. Because of this, more and more local governments are asking citizens to donate funds to support projects. Usually a city publishes a "wish list" of its needs, and citizens can select and pay for projects or items as gifts to the city.

Detroit calls its wish list a "Recreation Gifts Catalog." Detailed on the pages are a variety of recreation items and services, ranging from folding chairs for a recreation center at $10 apiece to a "share" in a $3.5 million renovation of a historic building for an arts complex. Detroit donors can also sponsor such activities as summer basketball camps, neighborhood Halloween parties, an annual Christmas carnival, senior citizen arts and crafts exhibits, and programs for the handicapped.

Parks and recreation centers are often the beneficiaries of city gift-givers. Even in wealthy Lake Forest, Illinois, a suburb of Chicago, citizens have been asked to donate funds to landscape parkways and to create an artificial lake within the city golf course.

In some cities donations are requested for practical items, not just the extras or luxuries. Local governments may need typewriters, duplicating and copying machines, and even paint and cleanup services. In Baltimore, for example, the seats in Memorial Stadium were scrubbed clean as part of the public's response to the city's wish list.

MORE MONEY-SAVING MEASURES

Besides adopting "user fees," contracting out some public services, and publishing wish lists, cities have also been forced to save money within traditional public-service areas. In law enforcement small and medium-size cities may share such support services as the use of crime laboratories, computerized record-keeping, communications systems for dispatching, and even police-dog training. This sharing is usually more economical than consolidating smaller police departments with larger metropolitan police systems.

Money-saving measures within a department might also be initiated. In Kansas City, Missouri, Police Captain Bob McAtee developed a cost-effective program to refurbish city police cars with at least 90,000 miles (144,000 km) on their odometers. Rather than sending the vehicles to a scrap yard, the police department has the cars completely overhauled at a cost of $4,200 apiece (mid-1983) compared with about $8,700 to buy a new car.

The refurbished vehicles handle and peform better than newly manufactured vehicles. "We have found that our refurbished cars have just as safe, predictable characteristics and long-range reliability as new models, and I can see this type of program as a viable concept for all public service agencies," McAtee said.

Other types of cost-cutting in city departments have been accomplished with automation, through better management or by using more efficient equipment. A sanitation department may buy new trash collection trucks that can be loaded from the curb rather than the rear. A curbside loader can be operated by a driver and one other worker, while the older rear-loading truck usually requires two workers along with the driver. Thus it is possible to cut back on the number of sanitation department employees. Another example of cost-cutting could be installing a computer system to save clerical charges for filing, billing, and other tasks.

Money-saving measures are as varied as the city department heads, local government officials, or city consultants who initiate ways to cut back city hall expenses. In recent years, however, many cities have been studying ways to manage energy more efficiently. Not only is this a conservation measure but it also helps bring about cost savings. In a few cities, energy man-

agement has become one of the functions of government.

Usually a city with an energy management program hires a coordinator who collects, analyzes, and distributes information about ways to conserve energy in the different city departments and operations. Energy conservation programs can include such projects as water and pollution control, pruning trees to provide better street lighting, paper recycling, and more efficient energy use in public buildings.

"Building-related energy comprises about half of all energy consumed within our cities," writes David Morris, president of the Institute for Local Self-Reliance in Washington, D.C., and an expert on energy use in urban America. Morris points out that building codes and regulations for land use can help a city become more energy-efficient. But building codes and land-use laws vary greatly from city to city. Most cities have to adopt building codes set or approved by the state. Unless a city has home rule, the state has to give permission to include energy efficiency as part of the city planning process. According to Morris, several states "require localities to consider the efficient use of energy as part of their comprehensive land-use plans."

City governments have tried to reduce their energy consumption in other ways. Some have purchased fleets of smaller cars for city use. Others have been able to cut energy use simply by locating and closing city-owned buldings that are vacant. A surprising number of city governments do not have good records or inventories of the empty buildings they own, nor do they know how much fuel they consume.

Lighting is "one of the major expenditures of city governments." As Morris points out, some northeastern cities "spend more than $10 per person per year for street lighting." But costs can sometimes be reduced by replacing mercury vapor lights with sodium lamps that use half as much electricity to produce about the same amount of light.

Whatever the methods of conserving energy (and cutting costs), the business of energy efficiency will concern local governments for some time to come. Transportation companies, building firms, and industries of many types are already involved in developing products that make better use of fuels. If fuel supplies are limited and the cost of energy continues to rise, cities will have to make use of more and more conservation measures.

At the same time some cities may look for ways to develop their own power plants and recycle an increasing number of goods. Cutting energy costs may be crucial to whether or not cities of the future are able not only to survive the cash crunch but also to maintain the limited resources needed to sustain life.

RUSTY RAILS, BUCKLING BRIDGES, AND SINKING STREETS

CHAPTER THREE

America's cities have been shaped by "a changing fuel base," writes energy expert David Morris. "When wood was supreme the cities were isolated villages. King Coal transformed them into giant industrial cities. Petroleum created the sprawling suburban cities."

While industries were developing in the nation, cities built up around factories where people worked. Horsedrawn cars on rails and the coal-powered electric streetcars of the late 1800s extended the growth of cities. People could live 5 to 10 miles (8 to 16 km) from city centers where jobs were and still get back and forth in a reasonable length of time. Railroads allowed cities to expand even further. From the early 1900s until after World War II, most freight was shipped by rail and more than two-thirds of the people who used public transit traveled on the railroads.

Then, in the 1950s, the pattern changed. Because of inexpensive fuel and convenience, the automobile became the favorite way to travel. Cheap fuel also helped bring forth the jet age. The federal government spurred both forms of transportation by financing airport development and interstate highway construction.

With the vast network of highways, the trucking industry was able to grow rapidly. Rail shipments dropped off; passenger service also declined. At the same time, urban transit systems were affected by the popularity of the automobile. Mass transit ridership declined by more than half between 1945 and 1960.

CHANGING REGULATIONS

Because large railroad companies used many unfair and illegal practices to control most of the rail transport in the late 1800s, the federal government passed laws that regulated the railroads strictly. Later, trucking and airline firms were also controlled by government agencies, but these transportation companies received subsidies or funds from the federal government. Thus, trucking and airline companies could charge lower rates than railroads for freight transport. Some railroads began to lose money and were forced out of business.

Federal controls on railroads, airlines, trucking, and even city bus services have been relaxed in recent years. Such deregulation has helped the railroads receive a fair share of the freight business. Passenger rail service has also been building up due to the establishment of the National Railroad Passenger Corporation, known as Amtrak. This private corporation, set up by Congress in 1970, is subsidized by the federal government and provides nationwide passenger service. Conrail, another private corporation supported by federal grants, was created in 1976 by consolidating six bankrupt railroads; it has revived rail service in the Northeast.

STALLED MASS TRANSIT

While national rail transport attempts a comeback, urban mass transit systems struggle to survive. Over the years mass transit fares have steadily increased, but they do not begin to cover the costs of operating buses and subways. And city governments have not been able to make up the shortfall in operating funds even though federal grants have provided for capital improvements.

Without the needed revenues, bus and subway maintenance suffers. Equipment becomes more decrepit and must be pulled from service, creating inconveniences for passengers and more congestion on transit lines. According to some estimates, about 25 percent of the nation's bus and subway systems now need to be replaced, at a total cost of $47.6 billion.

In New York City alone, just to begin rebuilding the ancient metropolitan transit system could cost more than $7 billion over a five-year period. Federal funds will help with replacement costs, but New York (like other cities) has to match funds. In the November 1983 elections, New Yorkers approved a $1.25 billion bond issue that will help finance the rebuilding of their city's infrastructure.

Added to the problem of deteriorating urban subways and other transit systems are the huge expenditures needed to create new ones. Los Angeles, for example, is hoping to build a countywide mass transit network that is expected to cost more than $3 billion when completed. During the summer of 1983, $127.5 million in federal construction funds was approved for the beginning of the high-speed rail and bus network.

One of the major new urban transportation systems:
San Francisco's Bay Area Rapid Transit (BART)
sleek trains leave a downtown station.

The first leg will be an 18-mile (28.8-km) subway line linking Los Angeles with North Hollywood, a high-density area that, according to the *Los Angeles Times*, "already absorbs more commuters every day than the entire San Francisco" subway system.

Subways are also under consideration for such cities as Houston, Seattle, and Honolulu. Voters in Houston, however, recently turned down a tax proposal to provide matching funds for a mass transit system. Thus the city lost all but $5.5 million of the total $110 million it would have received in federal aid for mass transit. Houston voters apparently did not believe a rail line would solve their traffic problems.

Robert W. Poole, Jr., a syndicated columnist and consultant to local government agencies, criticizes new rail systems because they do not save energy or reduce traffic congestion. "Surveys show that they [subways] attract more of their ridership away from buses. Thus, they do very little to reduce the number of cars on the road. And by depriving buses of riders, they serve only to worsen the dismal economics of existing bus systems," Poole claims.

On the other hand, some urban analysts argue that prospective benefits from subway systems could justify the high costs. Direct benefits can include less pollution, fewer accidents, more convenient and faster travel, and more "reserve capacity"—subways are designed to carry large numbers of passengers if a city grows and ridership increases.

Other benefits of a subway system are more indirect and seem to "ripple out," going well beyond the transport of people. Boris Pushkarev, an urban planner in New York, points to "a more compact pattern of urban development that a subway enables but cannot guarantee."

If dependable mass transit is available, companies may be encouraged to locate in urban centers where many unemployed people need jobs. More downtown business development means less need for overall travel, which saves considerable energy. More concentrated urban centers bring additional energy savings because less heat is lost from buildings that are close together, and infrastructure lines for sewer, water, telephone, electricity, and similar networks are more energy-efficient to build and maintain.

A recent urban study called *The Costs Sprawl*, sponsored by several federal government agencies, found that a low-density development such as a sprawling suburb would consume twice as much energy as a high-density *planned* community. Although energy savings are far from ideal in most cities today, the average city resident who makes use of mass transit consumes much less energy than someone living in a low-density area where the auto is the basic means of travel.

Whatever the relationship of energy-saving to density and mass transport, the problems of moving people are not confined to urban centers. Networks of roads and bridges are still vital to people who travel in and out of major cities. But many streets, expressways, bridges, and tunnels are crumbling.

BUCKLING BRIDGES

Striped barricades topped with blinking caution lights block the roadway. Bridge Out, a sign warns. it's a familiar scene in many cities. More than 3,500 bridges in the nation are closed, and hundreds of thousands are dilapidated or obsolete.

In just one metropolitan area—Chicago and its surrounding suburbs—at least 170 bridges need to be replaced, according to a November 1983 survey by the *Chicago Sun-Times.* A number of bridges handle only auto traffic and have been closed to trucks, tractors,

*Hairline cracks, discovered on Boston's Massachusetts
Avenue Bridge over the Charles River,
forced temporary closing of the two outside lanes.*

fire engines, and buses. Some have been declared "critically deficient" and have been closed off entirely.

Across the state of Illinois thousands of bridges are expected to need major overhauls in the near future. As in other parts of the nation, most bridges in Illinois were constructed during the 1920s and 1930s. Others were built even earlier when the horse and buggy were on the roads. Since the average life span for a bridge is fifty years, routine repairs are essential to prevent collapse. But over the past few years, the repair and maintenance of bridges have been put off due to lack of funds, the Illinois Transportation Department reports.

The story is the same in other states. With more bridges than any other state, Texas has over 18,000 that are obsolete or crumbling. A number of states have restricted the traffic on many of their bridges. Often there are weight limits or only one-way traffic is allowed. As long as drivers obey restrictions, bridges can be crossed without danger.

Most states pay close attention to bridge safety. At least once a year state inspectors check bridges on major roadways, looking for signs of stress such as cracks, rust, and noticeable sagging. But the *possibility* of life-threatening conditions exists when repairs are delayed.

There is some hope for the many bridges in disrepair. In January 1983 a nickel-a-gallon increase in the gas tax was signed by President Reagan, providing funds for bridge repair and replacement. The annual outlay for bridges will be a little over $2 billion.

Some street and highway departments benefit from the increased gas tax also. In 1983 interstate highways got the largest portion of funds at $1.7 billion and major U.S. routes received $600 million for repairs. Another $600 million was targeted for highway safety programs and miscellaneous road work.

Yet city streets are crumbling and cracking at a record rate. Many have been patched and repatched, and some need to be rebuilt. The total estimated cost for city street repairs is $600 billion. The interstate system and other federal highways need $952 billion. So the recent gas-tax funding, earmarked for street repairs, seems like a mere drop of asphalt in a gigantic nationwide pothole.

According to an April 1983 *Readers Digest* report by Ted Rakstis, the gas-tax funds are only a first step. He predicts "economic chaos" unless the nation begins "an all-out effort to rebuild not only the highways but nearly our entire transportation structure." Like others who have reported on our transportation woes, Rakstis cites the need for public and private funding that some experts believe could total over $4.5 *trillion* between 1983 and the year 2000.

SOLVING TRANSPORTATION PROBLEMS

In spite of high costs, a number of metropolitan areas are working on ways to keep their transportation supply lines open and flowing smoothly. Cities depend on networks of rails, roads, tunnels, bridges, and waterways to keep goods and people moving into and out of urban centers.

As mentioned in the previous chapter, an increasing number of people are sharing rides in car and van pools. And the concept is even being expanded in some areas. Manufacturing companies, businesses, and stores are providing vans or buses to pick up employees and customers as a way to ease traffic congestion and to transport people more efficiently and at lower cost. This idea could go further with "public vehicles"—cars and vans owned and operated by a city or town. Such community vehicles could take commuters to railroad or subway lines or to express bus stops, thus becoming part of the mass transit network.

Another cog in the mass transit network is the "light rail vehicle," or LRV. Something of a hybrid, the LRV is a cross between a trolley car and an interurban electric rail car. Trolleys and streetcars were the mainstay of urban transit systems until the 1940s, but the new LRVs, although similar in appearance to trolley cars, do not depend on overhead electric lines for power. Some can be recharged at passenger stops.

LRVs are already in use in San Diego, California, and Edmonton, Canada. Other cities such as Toronto, Canada; Buffalo, New York; Portland, Oregon; Denver, Colorado; and Los Angeles, California, are building light rail systems or have them on the drawing boards. Chicago is also making plans to use LRVs as a way to link its suburban areas with the city's major airport, O'Hare International. According to transportation experts, LRVs are less expensive to build than subway systems, which cost $150 million a mile. In contrast, LRV systems can be built for $15 to $30 million per mile.

Moving sidewalks and more streamlined buses are other modes of travel that are being developed in some cities to improve mass transit. Less conventional are magnetic-levitation trains, which hover above tracks and can travel at more than 250 miles (400 km) per hour. Such trains are being tested in Japan and Germany and may be developed in the United States to transport people along supercity corridors such as the area between Chicago, Illinois, and Milwaukee, Wisconsin.

Along with improvements in modes of travel, some efforts are under way to find practical and more economical methods to tie urban transport systems together. Major airlines, for example, provide transportation over long distances. But once on the ground, passengers have to connect with cabs, buses, trains, LRVs, or with other airlines to complete their trips.

If people travel by bus or train, they have few options at stations for other means of transport. Some experts believe that "intermodal" transportation centers are needed in big cities. From such centers bus lines, railways, subways, airport vans, limousines, and various shared-ride vehicles could branch out. The complex network of arteries—rails, roads, tunnels, subways, and bridges—might then be more convenient and useful to the millions of people moving themselves or goods in and out of urban areas. *87-16081*

WATER AND SEWER SYSTEMS

CHAPTER FOUR

Turn on the faucet and water flows. Countless times each day people across the
nation tap water supplies for drinking,
cooking, washing, cleaning, gardening, and
many other home uses. On the average the
nation consumes at least 150 gallons
(567.75 liters) of water per person daily.
Included in this average is water provided
for industries, stores, shops, offices, and
other business and public facilities. Both
personal and nonpersonal uses are taken
into account when determining the average
supply of water used in a community.

Most people in industrialized countries
take it for granted that water will flow when
faucets are turned on. But few think about
the sources of their water supply. Between
70 to 80 percent of the earth's surface is
covered by water, but that doesn't mean all
of it can be used. A vast amount of water is
found in salty oceans. Unless salt is

removed, the ocean water is unsuitable for people, animals, and plants that live on land. Just 1 percent of the earth's water supplies human needs, and that supply comes from freshwater lakes, rivers, streams and underground sources.

Some water sources dry up, but because of the *hydrologic* (water) cycle, water is never lost. It moves constantly by evaporation from surface waters (oceans, lakes, rivers, ponds) and land and by transpiration from plants into the atmosphere, moving back to the oceans and land to continue the cycle. All water at some time becomes vapor in the air. The water vapor cools, forming clouds and precipitation in the form of rain, snow, sleet, hail, dew, or fog. Some precipitation evaporates immediately and goes on with the water cycle. Some moisture, though, soaks into the ground and percolates through the soil to underground reservoirs. Groundwater moves slowly toward rivers and streams, eventually flowing into oceans.

WHAT IS A WATER SYSTEM?

While the supply of water is ever-present on earth, getting this supply to people is what water systems are all about. In some parts of the world people have to travel to public wells to fill containers with water and carry them back to their homes, as was common in ancient times. The early Romans, however, devised a system of aqueducts—stone troughs on archways above ground—that carried water from mountain springs to cities. Some of those aqueducts are still in use.

The first American cities were built near rivers or lakes to take advantage of the water supply, and many major U.S. cities such as Chicago, Pittsburgh, and St. Louis developed beside waterways. But a large number of cities, with no nearby surface waters, have had to drill wells and pump water from underground sources. Some cities, like New York and Los Angeles, pipe in water from storage reservoirs on rivers and lakes miles away.

Tapping a water supply may be fairly simple, but the system that treats and carries water to consumers in a big city can be complex. Since ancient times, people have boiled and filtered their water to make it taste and look better, but only in the mid-1800s did scientists discover that bacteria in water could cause diseases. Filtering can prevent many impurities from entering the water piped to consumers, but chlorine and other purifying materials help cleanse the water supply in most cities.

The water filtration plant in Chicago treats water for about three million people. The eight-hour process begins at the intake cribs, which sit about 2½ miles (4 km) from shore out in Lake Michigan. Tunnels in the bedrock under the lake carry water to a huge basin in the treatment plant. Water can also be taken into the basin at the shoreline. From there the water is pumped 20 feet (6 m) above the lake; purifying materials are added and mixed in; then the water flows into settling basins where impurities can sink to the bottom. The water then filters through sand and gravel, and, after another purification treatment, flows through tunnels to pumping stations and is finally piped to consumers.

In cities where wells pump water from underground sources, the treatment process is similar to lake (and river) purification systems. But what about the water that flows through the network of delivery pipes in city after city? Is all of that water really clean?

POLLUTED WATER SYSTEMS

Purifiers have eliminated waterborne bacteria that caused such killer diseases as typhus and cholera. But water today is often tainted by chemicals. The federal Environmental Protection Agency (EPA) recently estimated that as much as 30 percent of the nation's drink-

ing water contains traces of chemicals that can be linked to birth defects, cancer, and respiratory diseases.

A Safe Drinking Water Act, passed by Congress in 1974, authorizes the EPA to set strict national drinking water standards, which are enforced by state governments. Public water supplies must be tested often for contaminants, then purified if necessary. But since the 1974 Act, levels of pollutants—measured in parts per million, billion, and sometimes even trillion—have been set for only 20 chemicals, although some 700 chemicals have been identified in drinking water. Scientists say 129 of those chemicals may be toxic.

During the summer of 1983, more than fifty wells in Florida, for example, were closed because traces of a pesticide were found in the water. The ethylene dibromide (EDB) used to kill pests in citrus groves may also have seeped into underground reservoirs. In Florida and other states, drinking water has been contaminated not only by pesticides. Household cleaners, solvents from a variety of industries, road deicing salts, fertilizers, and other chemicals are polluting water supplies. The problem, as one researcher put it, is that when "you use a substance, no matter how innocent it is, it is going to show up in the water eventually."

Billions of dollars have been spent to control pollution in the water supply of North America and in other parts of the world. Factory wastes and sewage in waterways have decreased a great deal since the 1960s, when many lakes and rivers in industrialized countries were being choked by pollutants. Such poi-

Garbage, sludge, and sewage combine to pollute the waters of Lake Michigan at Montrose Harbor.

sons as DDT and mercury have been reduced. But now the presence of "micro-pollutants" in waterways is widespread, according to a 1972–1982 United Nations study on the world environment.

Erik Eckholm, who reports on environmental issues worldwide, says that toxic chemicals, metals, disease-causing microorganisms, and thermal pollution of waterways are the chief concerns. "In general, pollution from so-called point sources like sewage pipes and factories" is being controlled, Eckholm writes. "But the contamination of waterways from nonpoint, diffuse sources—runoff from farmlands, which tends to carry fertilizers, pesticides, and organic matter; and from urban areas, which often carries oil, metals, and other pollutants" appears to be on the increase in industrialized countries. "And acids and heavy metals falling with the rain constitute additional nonpoint sources of water degradation."

WATER SHORTAGES

"In another 50 years, more than half of the precipitation that falls to the earth's surface will be used for drinking water, agriculture, and mineral-resource development, compared with a fraction of that amount now. Even with new approaches to farming, there still will be stiff competition for usable water . . . supply lines may be lacking."

That is a prediction from the editors of *U.S. News and World Report* on the quality of life in the future. Some water-supply experts believe that conservation and recycling of water and developing technology will prevent severe water shortages. Others predict that desalinization techniques will be improved so that seawater can be used for human consumption.

At the present time, however, people in southern California's sprawling cities are often painfully aware that their water systems could run dry. With its low rainfall, southern California would be a desert without the water supply piped hundreds of miles from northern areas. The water systems that serve Los Angeles, San Diego, and many cities between are fed by a complex network of aqueducts, canals, ditches, and pumps. A major source of water has been the Colorado River, but since 1984 half of that supply has been diverted to parched Arizona cities.

Northern California has ample water resources in its lakes and rivers and from melting snows in mountain areas. For years California water planners have talked about diverting water from the northern part of the state to southern sections. One recent plan was to divert water from the Sacramento River, the state's largest, to southern California via a 42-mile (67.2-km) canal. But voters in northern California defeated a 1982 proposal for the "Peripheral Canal," as it has been called.

Henry Davis, writing for Friends of the Earth and others who oppose the canal, points out that the "42-mile (67.2-km) ditch" would bypass the Sacramento–San Joaquin Delta and drain off quality water and increase the salt water that could seep into this fertile area. Davis claims the canal could have been "a $23 billion boondoggle" that would have raised water bills and taxes, added to pollution, encouraged waste, and been of benefit to only big utilities and agribusiness.

Other critics of the canal believe that southern California water systems should be reclaiming waste water, and state officials should be promoting more efficient use of the water supply that now exists. Davis also suggests that more aggressive efforts be made to develop groundwater basins to store surplus water from wet years to be used during dry years. He suggests as well that "state-mandated conservation measures . . . [will] result in a drop of 14 to 17 percent" in the demand for southern California urban water by the year 2000.

Still, the Metropolitan Water District, which distributes water to cities and counties in southern California, is concerned about a water shortage. By the year 2000, at least three million more people will be living in southern California and the population of the entire state is expected to increase by more than ten million. Because so many cities in the Southwest are growing so rapidly, they will be hard-pressed to expand their water systems. Some geologists predict that groundwater supplies will run low, resulting in a migration of people back to northern states where water is plentiful.

"WASTE NOT, WANT NOT"

It is a familiar bit of advice. And conserving water is just as important in water-rich states as it is in drier areas. Water pipes have deteriorated in many cities, and water seeps or gushes away unused—wasted. During just one month in 1982, Milwaukee had 170 water-main breaks. Some cities like Scranton, Pennsylvania, lose nearly half of their daily water supply because of leaky pipes. Over a million gallons of water leak away each day in Berwyn, Illinois. During the hottest part of summer in 1982, residents of Jersey City, New Jersey, were without running water for five or six days. The cause? An over-eighty-year-old main burst, forcing a million gallons of water into streets instead of homes. People had to fill buckets with water from National Guard tankers brought in during the emergency.

Each year people consume (and waste) more and more water. According to some estimates, the nation will use more than a trillion gallons of water per day at the beginning of the next century. In spite of predictions that water shortages will be overcome, some experts believe that by the year 2000 the nation will run out of "portable" water—it will be impossible to get water to all of the people who will need it. Government reports say that "water is the most serious long-range problem confronting the nation—potentially more serious than the energy crisis."

To conserve part of the nation's water supply, much of it will have to be reused, according to an expert on water recycling, John R. Shaeffer, president of a Chicago engineering firm and adviser to local and federal governments on water pollution control. Shaeffer says, "Billions have been spent making sure we don't run out of water." But constantly searching for new water sources is not the solution to the water crisis, he insists, proposing instead that water be reclaimed along with the wastes it carries.

The concept seems simple enough, but the big obstacle is that "for 200 years people have been carefully taught to think negatively about wastewater or sewage," Shaeffer says. Recycling sewage is a subject many people find offensive, and few want to analyze wastewater from the standpoint of reclaiming it as drinking water.

Another problem with waste recycling is that most water system engineers in the United States have long advocated "linear water systems." That is, they see "water flowing in a straight line from sources to users to receiving streams and on out to sea." As Shaeffer writes in his book *Future Water*, people have believed that "the nation had enough water to serve indefinitely both as a water supply and to dilute municipal sewage discharged into streams and other natural bodies of water." If wastes could not be diluted, engineers have designed technological treatment systems to clean up the wastewater or sewage.

Dr. Shaeffer and many water system experts in Europe propose alternative water systems that make use of waste as a natural resource, as nature's way of cleansing water. With such a system, used water goes back into the soil, plants, and air and is recycled over and over again.

One pilot project for such a closed circular system,

as it is called, has been working "with great success for more than a decade in Muskegon County, Michigan," says the district's congressman, Guy Vander Jagt. Besides the highly industrialized city of Muskegon, a dozen other towns are served by a treatment system that moves wastewater out of waterways where it pollutes to the land where it adds nutrients to the soil.

The sewage is piped to "biological treatment cells," or lagoons, where floating churns help bacteria and oxygen begin the purification process while retaining the nitrogen, phosphorus, and potassium—primary fertilizers. Water then flows from the treatment cells to huge storage lagoons covering 1,700 acres (688 hectares). After additional treatment the nutrient-rich water is spray-irrigated onto crops such as field corn, which after harvest have returned over $1 million a year to the county. As the water passes through the soil, "living filters" purify it before it is collected in an underground network of drainpipes. The clean water then flows into streams that in turn help flush pollutants from lakes and other waterways, finally completing the cycle and becoming a source of drinking water.

Similar systems that recycle sewage have succeeded in other parts of the nation. But before such circular systems can be widely adopted in the United States, people have to overcome the notion that wastes have to be "out of sight, out of mind." In addition Shaeffer points out that officials in industries and governments with vested interests in wastewater systems have created formidable opposition to any change in traditional disposal plants. Farmers in some areas also resist the idea of recycling urban waste for soil nutrients. At the present time, Schaeffer and others who advocate wastewater recycling can only hope to pull together a coalition of supporters to help eliminate not only the water supply crisis but many pollution problems as well.

CLEANING UP

CHAPTER FIVE

Household garbage. Used paper and glass. Scrap metal. Rusted appliances. Junked cars. Industrial wastes. All kinds of throwaway materials are generated in urban areas. Collecting garbage and other trash is usually the responsibility of municipal sanitation departments in large cities. But private firms provide trash pickup services in many small cities and towns. And some urban areas use a combination of public and private services.

Whatever the system, refuse collection and disposal are of increasing concern to many city governments. In the first place, garbage collection is an expensive operation. New Yorkers generate about 20,000 tons of garbage daily. Collecting most of that trash (commercial garbage in New York is picked up by private haulers) costs the city about $210 million a year. Milwaukee has a budget of over $31 million annually for its sanitation department. In a smaller city like Birmingham, Alabama, the street and sanitation department spends about $13 million per year for services that include street maintenance along with other types of cleanup.

Some cities get by with much lower costs by using private firms that compete for collection services. The companies charge their customers directly, with no government involvement. In other instances city governments contract with private collectors and haulers or allow franchise operations—a private company is assigned to provide trash collection service in a certain section of the city, for fees paid by customers. Contract and franchise services may cost less because some municipal sanitation departments are not managed as efficiently as some private firms that have to make a profit. Because of union demands, for example, more employees might be hired by a city department than would be needed to accomplish the work. According to a mid-1970s Columbia University study of cities with populations between 2,500 and 750,000, cities with over 50,000 population spent 68 percent more for municipal garbage service than they would have spent by hiring the average contract firm to provide the same type of service. For cities below 20,000 population, the cost savings for private service were small.

WHERE TO STASH THE TRASH?

Besides cutting costs, city sanitation departments are faced with the more difficult and complex problem of

City garbage collection is fouled up here during a 1970s New York City garbage strike.

disposal. What can be done with tons and tons of daily garbage? In most cities garbage is burned or dumped at landfill sites, acres of land set aside especially for this purpose. About 10 to 15 percent of New York City's refuse is burned in incinerators. Only three of New York's thirteen incinerators are allowed to operate, however, since ten of them were designed and built before emission control standards were set by the federal Clean Air Act. Revamping all of the incinerators to control air pollution would be too costly.

Most of the refuse from New York City ends up in landfills. The largest in the world—3,000 acres (1,215 hectares)—is on Staten Island. After garbage is collected, it is hauled on trucks to marine transfer stations—special piers in Manhattan, Brooklyn, Queens, and the Bronx. Trucks dump the garbage onto barges that are pulled by tugboats to landfill sites. At the landfill the refuse is compacted by bulldozers and other heavy equipment.

As garbage compacts in any landfill, a liquid called leachate seeps out. Recent environmental regulations require that such seepage be treated to prevent groundwater contamination. Dump sites for toxic wastes have come under even more strict scrutiny and laws as the public and legislators have become more aware of the hazards of such materials.

HAZARDOUS DUMPS

Many people across the nation have heard about the notorious Love Canal toxic-waste site near Niagara Falls, New York. In 1980 the federal government relocated about 2,500 residents living nearby, because their homes and water supply were contaminated by leaks from the Love Canal site.

The Lipari landfill in Pitman, New Jersey; the LaBounty landfill at Charles City, Iowa; the Tar Creek landfill at Cherokee County, Kansas; the landfill at Somersworth, New Hampshire—the names are not familiar but they have the dubious distinction of being among the top twenty sites of the 148 on the EPA's priority cleanup list. In 1982 the EPA identified more than 400 toxic-waste sites across the country that needed immediate cleanup because of the health hazards.

In cities and counties across the land, toxic wastes from tanneries, the production of pesticides, paints, plastics, batteries, and hundreds of other products are a menace to citizens. According to a March 1983 *Newsweek* report, there are some 50,000 toxic-waste dumps in the United States plus "180,000 open pits, ponds and lagoons at industrial parks [that] bubble with witches' brews."

Thousands of these sites threaten groundwater supplies, are fire hazards, or emit fumes that could be health hazards. Recently the EPA estimated that the nation generates about 150 million metric tons of toxic wastes each year. Although Congress set aside $1.6 billion in 1980 to clean up toxic-waste sites, the EPA did not begin to assign any of that "superfund," as it is called, until late 1983.

Even with federal funding, cities and counties are having difficulty trying to get rid of hazardous wastes. States have to pay half the costs of cleaning up public property and 10 percent of cleanup costs on private land. Still, some states and large cities have set up agencies to investigate possible hazards of toxic wastes and bring to trial those who do not clean up or who dump poisonous materials illegally. In addition a number of private firms are beginning to get into the business of hazardous waste processing. More stringent environmental laws passed in the fall of 1983 require that toxic wastes be burned rather than dumped in landfills, so waste processors have been expanding their facilities to incinerate toxic materials.

RECYCLING REFUSE

Although there is increasing public opposition to any type of landfill, some cities have been able to tap their garbage disposal sites to recover resources such as glass and metals. Also, a number of cities are studying and beginning to implement ways to convert garbage into energy. Bulk-burning is one of the least expensive methods for turning garbage into steam, which can then be used to generate heat or electricity.

One of the first bulk-burning operations started in Saugus, Massachusetts, during the late 1970s. The Refuse Energy Systems Company (RESCO) burns about 1,200 tons (1,088 metric tons) of garbage a day. The refuse comes from two of Boston's districts and sixteen of its suburbs. Steam generated at RESCO is sold and piped to a nearby General Electric plant.

Similar operations are under study or functioning in other cities. But there are often political obstacles. People do not favor a recovery or a recycling facility any more than a landfill next door.

Mountain View, California, however, has fared well with its garbage disposal operations. In fact the city *imports* refuse from San Francisco, some 30 miles (48 km) away. The imported trash is used to fill a floodplain that will eventually become a golf course with an adjacent gas refinery. A covered landfill (which is what the golf course will be) can produce a natural gas called methane. Wet organic matter decomposes, and the methane that results can be purified and piped into systems serving home heating and cooling needs. A num-

City-collected refuse is processed in a Milwaukee, Wisconsin, recycling plant.

ber of cities and towns in the San Francisco Bay area receive their supply of natural gas from the Mountain View landfill source.

Other cities in various parts of the nation are finding that refuse recycling can be beneficial. As David Morris put it in his study, *Self-Reliant Cities:*

"A city of two hundred thousand annually throws away the amount of copper produced by a small copper mine, the amount of aluminum taken from a modest bauxite deposit, and as much paper as comes from a medium-sized timber stand." Morris points out that millions of tons of municipal waste are usually thrown away in a mass. But because recycled products are becoming more valuable, in some cities trash is separated by the type of material. "Several paper companies have already announced that future plants will be built only in communities that recycle aggressively," Morris says.

PARK AND RECREATION SYSTEMS

CHAPTER SIX

At the turn of the century, architects and writers were describing their cities (and U.S. cities in general) as "ugly," "vulgar," "chaotic," "undignified," and "tasteless." A near-crusade was under way to convince Americans that they should try to improve urban life. Urban planners wanted to make their cities more beautiful in design and style.

It was the "City Beautiful" movement, and it helped bring about the idea that cities should have open spaces—parks and plazas, broad streets, and boulevards lined with greenery. Another thrust of the movement was to develop "comprehensive planning" and zoning to control the use of land.

Besides setting aside park and recreation areas, some sections of the city would be residential, while others were zoned for business and for industrial use. The main purpose of early zoning was to plan for organized growth so that a city would not develop in a haphazard manner and could expand its infrastructure in an orderly way. Today zoning regulations in many cities have been amended to take into account the increasing interest in the preservation of historic areas and buildings, and conservation of the natural environment.

REVIVING WATERFRONTS

America's major cities grew up along waterways that provided the basic form of transport until railroads and later superhighways and airlines came along. As transportation systems changed and expanded, the nation no longer depended primarily on port facilities. Many old waterfront areas, which had been centers of commerce, were abandoned. Along with central-city areas, waterfronts were left for several decades to deteriorate.

In recent years, however, the picture has been changing again. City planners, government officials, and private-citizen groups have taken an interest in revitalizing waterfront areas as commercial and recreation centers. One of the most successful restoration projects is Boston's Faneuil Hall Market and Waterfront Park. The area includes renovated brick and granite buildings that contain shops and restaurants, marinas, an aquarium, and a park site for picnics, strolling, jogging, and similar activities. During the first year of its operation in 1976, the state received over $2 million in taxes from commercial sales, while the city's share was $225,000. Revenues have steadily increased, as an estimated 15 million people visit the area each year.

New Jersey's Liberty State Park along the Hudson River, Harborplace in Baltimore, the Riverfront Esplanade in Savannah, Georgia, the Moon Walk on the Mississippi River in New Orleans, Cannery Row on the

Baltimore, Maryland's reclaimed Harborplace is a prime example of inner city renovation and reuse.

coast in San Francisco—these are just a few of the waterfronts that have been revived.

Such projects are financed with a combination of private investments and grants from federal, state, and local governments. Funding is a major concern, but it is just one of the many problems urban planners must solve when trying to revamp a waterfront area. A master plan has to be created as part of the first stage.

A PARK IN THE MAKING

In Indianapolis, Indiana, the 260-acre (105-hectare) White River State Park project got under way in 1980–81 with designs created by eight well-known planning firms with offices in Los Angeles, Washington, D.C., New York City, Cambridge, Massachusetts, and New Haven, Connecticut. The master plan was developed around the concept of injecting new life into the city.

Indianapolis leaders and state officials hope to attract tourists, provide jobs, and develop the park as an asset to the state as well as the metropolitan area. With a population of 1.2 million, Indianapolis wants to change its sleepy image of "Naptown" (the nickname used by natives and visitors alike) to a more wide-awake, exciting scene. The goal is to make White River Park one of the Midwest's major year-round tourist attractions, to include a huge amusement complex, museums, a cultural center, a winter garden, a marina, and a zoo.

As the $200 million construction project—expected to be completed about 1990—got under way, land for the park site along both sides of the White River had to be cleared. The area is one of the oldest industrial sections in the city, with empty warehouses, abandoned factories, and old railyards. Much of the property was sold to the Park Commission, an agency set up by state law to create parklands. But some companies within

coast in San Francisco—these are just a few of the waterfronts that have been revived.

the park site have refused to sell their property to the commission since the firms are still in business. In such cases the commission has the power of *eminent domain*—the court can order the sale of property for public use, guaranteeing a fair price to the owners. Or the commission can decide to build the park around a business.

The second option was the commission's choice in regard to the huge Acme-Evans flour mill in Indianapolis. Not only would moving costs have been too high, but the facility has historical and educational value where it is. At least that is the opinion of a park task force headed by Patrick Horsbrugh, former chairman of the University of Notre Dame department of architecture.

Dr. Horsbrugh believes the mill, built in 1821, should be preserved, since it "is the oldest continuously operating enterprise in Indiana." The mill also represents the importance of the White River to the city's industry and the state's importance to the nation's soft wheat production. Another historic building, the water pumping station, has been restored as a visitors' center within the park site.

One of the most controversial aspects of the park is the planned 750-foot (225-m) high Indiana Tower, designed by the well-known architect Cesar Pelli of New Haven, Connecticut. Pelli likens his creation to the Eiffel Tower on the Seine River in Paris. But critics have labeled the proposed concrete-and-limestone archways that pyramid toward the heavens the Awful Tower. One Indianapolis resident says the design looks like "a giant corn cob with all the grains gone." But there is little doubt the tower will be built if funds are available. As Pelli says, the tower is a "marker for the Plains," symbolizing openness and grass-roots democracy. But, just as important, the tower has been designed to attract attention, to draw people to the park.

The new White River Park and similar waterfront projects are much more than tourist attractions and commercial centers. They are city-oriented parks with many open, green spaces that city planners worldwide believe are important to the quality of life in urban areas.

But what about maintaining older park and recreation systems? Can cities afford them? Do urban people really use their parks? What effect do they have on a city?

These are just a few of the questions that face city park and recreation departments. A former administrator for New York City parks, August Heckscher, says that a city's park system "is the arena for recreation, active and passive. . . . If the city is something more than a static place, it must be the forum in which transactions and celebrations occur; there must be open spaces that provide a fitting stage for the drama of daily life."

In the midsection of the nation, park officials in Omaha, Nebraska, do not use such metaphors, but they believe "Omaha's park and boulevard system is one of its most valuable assets." The officials point out that "America has undergone a series of changes in regard to parks during the last century. Initially, the urban park was a quiet retreat, a restful place to escape the noise and confusion of the city. Boulevards were an integral part of the system, connecting the parks and providing a means for walking and driving to view the beauty of the landscape."

After World War II most parks became sites for recreational activities. But recently the scene has changed again. People have increasingly been seeking quiet retreats within the densely populated areas where they live.

Planners in Oxnard, one of southern California's most rapidly growing cities, see parks and recreation facilities as "essential" to urban life. Oxnard planners recommend a standard of 10 acres (4 hectares) of open space—in the form of state, city, or neighborhood parks—per 1,000 people.

PAYING FOR PARKS AND OTHER LEISURE SERVICES

Few cities can boast such an extensive string of waterfront parks—green and clean—as Chicago. Besides parks along the shore of Lake Michigan, the city also has many other well-kept parks and wooded preserves within its system. But the Chicago Park District "stands out as the big spender of the park world," according to a fall 1983 investigation by the *Chicago Sun-Times*. The newspaper computed the cost per acre to operate city park agencies in Chicago at about $15,500 per year.

In contrast, Detroit spends about $7,300 per acre annually; New York's cost is $5,000; Los Angeles spends about $3,200; Dallas, a little over $1,800; and San Diego has an annual cost per acre of $1,200 to operate its parks. The total annual budget for the Chicago Park District is $113.5 million. Only New York City has a higher budget—$125 million—but the park acreage in New York is three times that of Chicago.

Why the big differences in park spending? The *Sun-Times* reports that there are far too many employees in Chicago's Park District, and many people are on the payroll because of the patronage system—jobs are offered as a kind of reward or payment for political loyalties. Some Park District officials insist that Chicago has an unusually large number of indoor recreational facilities, and the District is also responsible for parks adjacent to schools, which boost costs. But many park experts across the nation believe that the heavy patronage leads to inefficiency and wastes tax money.

To cut costs for parks and recreation services, a number of cities have contracted with private firms to maintain park grounds, median strips along boulevards, and landscaped areas around public buildings. User fees also help with costs. The fees come in many forms, such as admission fees to amusement parks, campgrounds, swimming pools, zoos, museums, parking garages, and other public facilities. Fees for licenses and permits to fish, boat, or hunt are other sources of revenue for park departments.

"Adopt-a-Park" programs also help cut expenses. In Detroit, "adoption papers" are made out for groups willing to care for a park, playlot, or playground. Usually neighbors—whether in business or residential areas—band together and paint equipment, cultivate shrubs and flowers, clean up debris, and generally make the park or play area more esthetically pleasing.

Park support groups operate across the nation from Oakland, California, to New York City. Similar volunteer groups help maintain public zoos, libraries, and museums. Advocates of privatization believe local governments should get out of the business of operating leisure services, allowing volunteers and commercial firms to manage such activities. Some cities now require construction firms that build new housing developments to include parks, schools, and other public facilities. The costs for such facilities are added to the price of homes and passed on to buyers.

Yet there is serious debate about who should be responsible for parks and open spaces in the cities. According to urban experts, open spaces often shape a city and create its unique character. Thus planners, environmentalists, and other concerned citizens believe that open spaces—including parks, waterfront areas, and even mountains within city limits—need to be preserved and maintained by local governments for the benefit of the city as a whole.

CONNECTING WITH THE CENTRAL CITY

Just as waterfronts in many older cities were neglected for decades, so were downtown areas. Since downtown is often next to or part of a waterfront, reviving an area along a waterway nearly always includes an attack on downtown decay. City planners and local officials want to see downtowns connect again with the rest of the urban network.

Omaha, Nebraska, is one city that has taken on the challenge of both riverfront and major downtown revival. Since the early 1970s, the city has been constructing its Central Park Mall, most of which was completed by 1982, with the final section of the mile-long park and shopping area to be finished in the late 1980s.

The block-wide mall—with paved plazas, grassy slopes, trees, and water tumbling over terraces into a large lagoon where goldfish and ducks swim—is the link

*Downtown Detroit's Renaissance Center
has proved a key factor in the new, appealing
look of a major city's downtown area.*

from downtown to the Missouri River. Boardwalks, footpaths, mini-cliffs made of sandstone blocks, and even a double slide 35 feet (10.5 m) long that sends kids and adults alike swooping into a huge sandy area are all part of the setting.

Major hotels, office buildings, department stores, and downtown housing have been renovated or developed in the blocks near the mall. As one of Omaha's planners pointed out, there has been "a collective, positive spirit"—business, government, and private groups have worked together to make things happen. Many Omaha residents feel their downtown is becoming a vital center of commerce again.

Other cities as diverse as Memphis, Tennessee; Louisville, Kentucky; Portland, Oregon; and San Diego, California, have been attempting similar types of revival. To make urban centers work again, citizen involvement and good planning are essential, civic leaders say. Tax incentives are needed also to make business development as attractive in aging city cores as it is in the suburbs. Cooperation between central city and suburban governments and leadership from city officials are other important factors that help pave the way to downtown rebirth.

LIVING DOWNTOWN

A downtown residential base is another mandatory element for the revival of the central city, experts insist. If people are downtown only during business hours, "the streets roll up after 5 P.M.," says Mayor Harvey Sloane of Louisville, Kentucky. Developers in Louisville predict a boom in downtown housing in that city through the rest of the 1980s. A number of major apartment complexes are planned, since many singles and middle-aged and retired couples, who make up the majority of returning urban dwellers, need places to live.

Interest in moving downtown has been sparked in cities from Baltimore, Maryland, to Savannah, Georgia, to Indianapolis, Indiana, to Portland, Oregon. Where people were once eager to move out of the central city to the suburbs, some are now going back. Convenience is a main attraction of downtown living. People like being near their jobs, shopping, public transportation, and such amenities as theaters, libraries, museums, and recreational facilities.

Many urban dwellers are moving into apartments and condominiums converted from old factory and warehouse space. Architects call the practice, which has been spreading in Chicago, St. Louis, Denver, and other urban areas, "adaptive reuse." The abandoned buildings can be renovated for offices, shops, or housing at a much lower cost than new construction, which some developers say could be ten times higher.

Thanks to revival efforts in many city downtowns, new hotels and restored hotels on a grand scale are bringing travelers to city centers once again. From 1948 to 1978, more than 17,000 hotels closed their doors in the nation's cities. Most of the hotels were in decaying downtowns, and travelers preferred more convenient and less expensive motel lodging off the interstates and other major highways. Many deluxe grand hotels that had served the famous and wealthy became shabby relics or were modernized so that they lost their original beauty and identity. Some were torn down and replaced with new structures.

A famous Washington, D.C., landmark, the Hotel Willard is in the process of being restored to its former luxury.

Just before the nation's Bicentennial, federal tax laws were changed to allow tax credits for restoring and preserving historic buildings. At the same time, construction costs were soaring so that it became less expensive to restore old hotels than to build new ones. Since 1976 dozens of historic hotels, such as the elegant Seelbach in Louisville and the Olympic in Seattle, have been brought back to life.

INNER-CITY JOBS

While downtown renovation may put a new face on a city, it does not necessarily mean jobs for inner-city neighborhoods that encircle, are next to, or form part of the core. Gary, Indiana, which is adjacent to the Chicago metropolitan area, boasts a new downtown convention center, a restored hotel, new streetlights, and an improved infrastructure with repaired roads, curbs, and sanitation system. But few of Gary's 150,000 residents benefit from their renovated downtown. In the midst of the 1981–82 recession, Gary's unemployment rate of 16 percent was six points higher than the national average.

The economy of the city depends a great deal on the steel industry, which has been in a slump nationwide. About a third of the 21,000 steelworkers in Gary and the surrounding areas were laid off in the early 1980s. Many other types of jobs have also been lost as retailers and banks have moved out.

One plan for restoring economic vitality to inner-city areas such as Gary has been touted by two New York congressmen, Republican Jack Kemp and Democrat Robert Garcia. Their proposal for "enterprise zones" is designed to provide federal tax credits and eliminate some federal taxes "to encourage new businesses to locate and grow in distressed inner-city neighborhoods, and hire and train economically disadvantaged individuals." Along with the federal program, local and state governments will be required to offer incentives such as improving the infrastructure of the depressed area. The main purpose of the program, Congressman Garcia says, is "to create jobs, spur private investment, and strengthen local economies."

The plan calls for either state or local governments to identify areas as enterprise zones. Such areas "would have to be characterized by distress, pervasive poverty, and high unemployment," Garcia says. Once an area has been nominated, state and local contributions to the enterprise zone would be taken into consideration to determine whether federal tax credits would be allowed. Applicants would be evaluated by the Department of Housing and Urban Development (HUD). Twenty-five enterprise zones would be selected annually, with a maximum of seventy-five authorized over a three-year period.

SAFETY AND HEALTH HAZARDS?

Along with the lack of jobs, many inner-city residents have to face the very real problem of violent crime, even though the overall crime rate for the nation dropped by 3 percent in 1982. According to FBI reports, violent crimes such as murder, rape, and robbery declined in New York, Philadelphia, Baltimore, Boston, and San Francisco. But serious crime increased in other cities, including Chicago and Detroit, although the rates of increase in those cities were not as high as some in the Sunbelt. Houston's crime rate from 1970 to 1982 soared by 112 percent, while the rate of increase for the same period was 127 percent in San Diego. Serious crime has also risen sharply in Los Angeles and is higher than New York, where there are many more people per square mile.

High crime rates have often been linked with overcrowding or high density. But there is no evidence to support the idea that overcrowding *in itself* leads to crime, according to Jonathan Freedman, chairman of the Department of Psychology at the University of Toronto. As a matter of fact, Dr. Freedman states: "Characteristics of cities, such as large populations, high density living, high activity level, and high noise level, are not associated with high crime rates." Instead, Dr. Freedman says there are many other causes of crime, such as poverty, lack of education, unemployment, and racial discrimination—characteristics that happen to concentrate in cities.

Many of the 12,000 residents of Overtown, a black neighborhood that is part of downtown Miami, would agree. Unemployment in the area is estimated at 40 percent, and about 25 percent of Overtown's residents are on welfare. Poverty hangs over the area like a shroud. People often sit idly on porches all day or gather in bars or video arcades. Many buildings were burned out during rioting that erupted in 1982 after a six-month period during which five blacks were killed by white police.

Many residents of Overtown believe that Miami police constantly hassle blacks, especially teenagers. In fact, the conflicts between the police and blacks in Overtown have been reported so often that the stories have almost become legends. The fear of police along with joblessness and hunger are never-ending threats to most of the Overtown residents. Few have much hope for change, since—as one black resident put it—black neighborhoods are not seen "as part of the community." Most blacks in Miami feel they have no power and have resigned themselves to living with violent crime and slum conditions, although some city officials insist economic improvements will be made in Overtown, and efforts are under way to relieve tensions between police and black citizens.

While poverty and crime are real concerns to inner-city residents, research shows that the majority of urban dwellers "are just as healthy physically, mentally and socially as those who live elsewhere," according to Dr. Freedman. Good health may depend more on how people live than where they live. Whether rural or urban, the poor have a greater possibility of becoming ill than middle-income people. Certain occupations and professions, such as teaching and the clergy, appear to add years to a person's life while blue-collar workers have shorter life spans. People who suffer the highest rate of lung disease are miners and smelters, most of whom do not live in big cities. Diet, exercise, work satisfaction, heredity, and even family ties seem to make more of a difference in health patterns than whether people live in cities or rural areas.

WHY THE "BAD RAP" FOR CITIES?

Although some studies conclude that parts of most American cities are safe and healthy, many rural people cling to the idea that cities are evil, filthy, fearful places. How did cities get such a bad reputation? If cities are such dreaded "dens of iniquity," why do 75 percent of the American people live in urban areas?

The bad name for cities may date back to ancient times. From the beginning of recorded history, people have described the lure of cities along with their revulsion for urban excesses. The ancient cities of Sodom and Gomorrah drew thousands of people inside their walls. But biblical stories catalog a variety of evils in the two cities whose names have become synonymous with wickedness and urban corruption.

In more recent history, America's early cities were thought to be havens for "mobs." People were suspicious of cities and preferred the wide open spaces, the forests, or the lush green countryside. According to a number of early American thinkers, simple rural life was supposed to be virtuous. People living on farms were thought to be self-sufficient; they could provide for their own basic needs—food, water, shelter, and clothing. City dwellers, on the other hand, were labeled dependent and subservient by President Thomas Jefferson.

Independence, ingenuity, self-reliance, and solitude were considered ideal characteristics by some American writers and leaders of the eighteenth and early nineteenth centuries. As Alfred Kazin, professor of English at City University of New York, explained recently in *Heritage* magazine, those who hated the cities feared "the influx of ignorant masses, their lack of manners, their lack of standards." Professor Kazin points out: "Although Americans are [now] more than ever an urban people, many . . . still think of the city as something it is necessary to escape from." He believes the fear of cities "is concern with class" or fear of the "underclass."

Living in the heart of New York City, Professor Kazin knows firsthand the threat of violence but says he could not live and work elsewhere. "I welcome every kind of freedom that leaves others free in the city," he writes. "The endless conflict of races, classes, sexes is raucous but educational. No other society on earth tolerates so many interest groups, all on the stage at once and all clamoring for attention."

A CHAPTER
NETWORK EIGHT
OF
NEIGHBORHOODS

People who live in a major urban center seldom think of their city in terms of a restored downtown or a rebuilt infrastructure. Instead most big-city residents identify with their neighborhoods, the blocks or streets where they live. To many urban dwellers, their neighborhood *is* the city. It is a place where they can sometimes share a way of life or feel part of a community.

In Los Angeles, for example, one neighborhood surrounded by downtown buildings is the center of southern California's Japanese community. Called Little Tokyo, the area is the hub of Japanese cultural and business activities. Chicago has its well-defined Irish, German, Chinese, Hispanic, and black neighborhoods. "Poletown" has long been a part of Detroit. And Ybor City, a district in Tampa, Florida, is a mix of ethnic neighborhoods.

Ethnic neighborhoods—urban areas settled by people of one cultural group—have always been part of the fabric of big cities in the United States. New York, a port of entry for hundreds of thousands of immigrants, has a network of ethnic neighborhoods, ranging from older communities like Chinatown and Harlem to the more recent "Little India." Almost a quarter of all New Yorkers were born in other countries.

For many immigrant groups, the city—whether New York, Chicago, Detroit, Los Angeles, or Tampa—has symbolized America. Newcomers are often able to get a start in urban centers. People settle in neighborhoods where relatives, friends, or other sponsors can pave the way, steering the new arrivals to jobs, homes, and schools, and helping immigrants overcome language barriers.

Brooklyn, once an independent city and now a borough of New York City, has been home for people from almost every cultural group in the world. During the 1800s, neighborhoods were populated by the Dutch, Irish, and Germans. The largest Jewish center in the nation developed in Brooklyn during the early part of this century. Hispanics, Italians, and Scandinavians settled in their own neighborhoods. In recent years there has been an influx of Chinese, Russians, and Poles. And a growing number of Brooklynites have arrived from Trinidad, Haiti, Jamaica, Panama, and Guyana. Along with African and other foreign-born blacks, American blacks have settled Brooklyn neighborhoods such as Crown Heights and Bedford-Stuyvesant.

Like many urban areas nationwide, some of Brooklyn's neighborhoods are getting face-lifts. In other sections of New York, however, such as the Bronx, neighborhoods are in deep trouble. They look like war zones, with crumbling buildings, graffiti-scarred walls, burned-out cars, and littered streets.

DECLINE AND FALL
OF NEIGHBORHOODS

Why do some older urban neighborhoods revive while others waste away or become urban jungles? Like waterfronts and downtowns in older cities, neighborhoods suffer because of diminishing funds, neglect, and the migration of people to the suburbs of the growing urban centers of the Southwest. Yet the decline of some neighborhoods is also due to a more complex set of problems.

A neighborhood is a mini-network within a city, made up of interrelated parts including homes, businesses, parks, schools, streets, and all the rest of the infrastructure. Often a whole neighborhood can be adversely affected when just one part of the network begins to deteriorate. Robert Cassidy, an urban expert and neighborhood conservationist who views neighborhoods as ecosystems, puts it this way: "As with a delicate coastal wetland, altering any of the many variables that are functioning as an interrelated whole can either make a neighborhood a healthy place to live or a stagnant environment that reeks of decay."

One of the factors that has altered the ecosystem in some city neighborhoods is government policy, from the federal to the city-hall level. Federal tax laws, for example, have favored new construction over the rehabilitation of older buildings. Builders have thus been able to get a better return on their investments by concentrating on new buildings, which are more often constructed in suburbs than in city centers. On the local level a city government may cut back services in poor neighborhoods, where residents have less political power to demand various services than people in affluent neighborhoods.

Sometimes new construction has been planned for the urban core through federal programs. Decayed buildings have been bulldozed to the ground, leaving wasteland or piles of debris in their place. Perhaps no new investors are willing to rebuild housing and businesses in the area. Or maybe the buildings were cleared for a new expressway financed by federal and state funds and pushed through by government officials regardless of the wishes of residents. People who once lived and worked in such areas have been unable to stop the razing of their neighborhoods.

Even though living conditions may be deplorable in some urban neighborhoods, where can people go if crumbling apartment buildings and homes are torn down? Possibly they will move to a nearby neighborhood. As a result the neighboring area could become overcrowded and run-down. Traffic may increase, creating congestion, pollution, and safety hazards, all of which could (but may not necessarily) lead to neighborhood decline.

In some urban areas "redlining" plays a part in bringing about the fall of a neighborhood. This practice began several decades ago when federal officials marked city maps with red lines to show neighborhoods that were not eligible for insurance from the Federal Housing Administration (FHA), which guaranteed loans for home mortgages.

Redlining has long been prohibited by law, but banks and other lenders have followed very similar procedures. An insurance company might increase rates, and some financial institutions may refuse loans for homes in neighborhoods considered risky. Lenders may charge higher interest rates or demand larger down payments for home mortgages in so-called "high risk" areas. Many banks refuse to make mortgage loans on property valued below a certain amount. Thus a home selling for $20,000 would not be eligible for a mortgage if the lender would not accept loans under $30,000. Since low-priced homes are usually in older neighborhoods, such homes may stay on the market, deteriorate from neglect, and contribute to the decay of a block.

Another important factor affecting neighborhoods is the way residents feel about their home area and how others perceive the neighborhood. If many people in a neighborhood are in constant fear of violent crime, they may be too distrustful and too afraid to work together for change. Fearful residents may move to neighborhoods that they believe are safe.

Sometimes a neighborhood has a bad reputation, the image of being a high-crime area. But the statistics may prove otherwise. Even so, people who do not live in the area will avoid the neighborhood if they believe it is crime-ridden. This in turn could have adverse effects such as cutbacks in city services and fewer mortgage loans, as just described, contributing further to neighborhood decline.

BLOCK GROUPS

Neighborhood action groups often play vital roles in attempts to stop urban decay, as has been proven in Brooklyn. While some of Brooklyn's neighborhoods may need a miracle to revive them, others have been restored and are dotted with boldly painted signs: God Bless Our Block. Such messages demonstrate that a city block or neighborhood has become a focal point for activists who care about the quality of their immediate environment.

What happens, though, when a block or neighbor-

Neighborhood associations often sponsor block parties and fairs to create a sense of community.

hood association goes to work? Prayers for a blessing may be part of the action, but mortals have to take the necessary steps to make changes.

Hattie Carthan, of Brooklyn's Bedford-Stuyvesant area, led the way in restoring her Vernon Avenue neighborhood. Homes had deteriorated because families lost jobs and could not afford to maintain their property. Hattie spent countless hours convincing neighbors to set up a volunteer group that would help to beautify Vernon Avenue.

One of the first group projects was raising funds for trees that were planted along the street. During the beautification effort, Hattie was able to save a rare magnolia tree in the neighborhood and quickly became known as the Magnolia Tree Lady. But her neighborhood action went much further. Under Hattie's guidance, the block association sought support from local businesses and applied for federal funds to get a major restoration project under way. A commercial center, which includes an ice rink and the Billie Holiday Theater, opened in 1975. Even a small manufacturing company has been built nearby to provide jobs for some 400 residents.

The restored neighborhood in Brooklyn is just one of the many grass-roots efforts to improve living conditions in urban America. In most major cities, block groups or neighborhood associations are donating services and materials that their financially strapped local governments are no longer able to provide. Neighborhood organizations are also setting up cooperatives to buy and sell food and heating fuel at low prices for members. In addition block groups provide crime-watch services, offer emergency plumbing and electrical work, and even set up real-estate offices, credit unions, and centers for alcoholics.

Although many cities shy away from neighborhood action, some urban officials believe neighborhood groups can bring real benefits to a city. As one city manager explained, neighborhood volunteer groups are able to provide services at "lower costs [and] are closer to citizens . . . if they aren't delivering, their neighbors can say 'hey, what's going on?' " More than 10,000 neighborhood associations nationwide are tackling jobs that may not bring about dramatic change, but can at least be first steps toward stopping urban decay.

NEIGHBORHOOD HOUSING

Those involved with neighborhood volunteer work believe that people who have vested interests in their neighborhoods will take better care of them. In Baltimore, for example, a volunteer neighborhood group has taken over the job of housing and vacant-lot inspection in some forty neighborhoods. Due to budget cuts, the city has had to lay off a third of its 100 inspectors since 1977. As a result many home- and landowners were not cited for violations of health and safety codes.

Volunteers now patrol neighborhoods to note debris-littered lots or buildings that are deteriorating. The neighborhood associations then send a list of health and safety hazards to property owners. Some resent the volunteer efforts, but neighborhood associations report that nearly 85 percent of the violators take care of needed cleanup and/or repairs. If property owners do not comply within thirty days, the city initiates legal action in the courts.

The volunteer efforts in Baltimore are part of the Neighborhood Housing Services (NHS) program, which promotes a variety of housing rehabilitation nationwide. "A private non-profit corporation, NHS brings together residents of a neighborhood, city officials and members of local financial institutions," explains Al Wojciechowski, president of the Broadway-Fillmore Neighborhood Housing Services in Buffalo, New York. "A city inspector with the NHS staff inspects each house on every block within a NHS neighborhood, checking for compliance with minimum health and safety standards. Then a housing specialist may help homeowners get cost estimates for repair work, provide counseling to help homeowners get loans or other funds to pay for improvements, or simply offer advice on proper home maintenance," Wojciechowski says.

Nearly 140 cities across the nation have NHS programs. NHS works closely with the Neighborhood Reinvestment Corporation, a public corporation chartered by Congress, which provides the technical support for local NHS staffs. The local NHS organizations also work with the National Neighborhood Housing Services of America to tap loan funds backed by major investors such as The Equitable Life Assurance Society of the United States, Prudential Life Insurance Company, and Aetna Life and Casualty Insurance Company. The loan funds provide financing for home improvements and mortgages if homeowners in NHS neighborhoods cannot borrow from a bank or other lending institution.

In Kansas City, Missouri, the NHS program is part of a citywide effort to preserve neighborhoods that has been under way since the late 1970s. Recently three Kansas City neighborhoods became part of a program called Partnership in Neighborhood Service Delivery. Administered by the city's Office of Housing and Community Development (OHCD), the program was granted federal and local funds to hire two neighborhood improvement specialists. Like their counterparts in Baltimore, the specialists will evaluate homes (just as city inspectors have done) and make recommendations for any improvements needed.

Mrs. Icelean Clark, director of the Partnership Program in her neighborhood, says, "We're hoping that by having one individual . . . be responsible for looking at a full range of problems, we can more effectively and efficiently upgrade a neighborhood. In the past, some neighbors may have felt harassed by having more than one person check for housing compliance, trash, weeds and rodents." The Kansas City OHCD director agrees, adding, "We hope that the neighborhood specialist will be looked upon as supportive . . . not as a city inspector who is dragging people into court."

HISTORIC PRESERVATION

Another type of neighborhood revival has been making headway since the 1970s. Neighborhood groups and individual property owners in some urban areas have become involved in preserving historic buildings. In the older eastern cities, street after street of brownstones—named for the reddish brown sandstone blocks used to build the homes—have been refurbished. These three or more story buildings were constructed during the 1800s as single-family homes for people in the upper and middle income brackets. During the Depression years in the 1930s, many homeowners had to divide their brownstones into apartments or take in roomers to help provide income. Some of these homes were poorly maintained or were allowed to fall apart from neglect.

In recent years, however, as in the restored Brooklyn neighborhood of Bedford-Stuyvesant, people have discovered not only the historic value of the buildings but also a type of architecture and design that cannot be found in homes built today.

Some urban neighborhoods have been designated as historic areas or districts by the National Register of Historic Places or by a state historical society. Often neighborhoods with such historic designations have reversed their decline and have seen their property values rise considerably. But historic preservation of a neighborhood is no easy or simple project.

In Ybor City, a historic section of Tampa, Florida, civic groups have been active since the 1970s trying to preserve the area's unique ethnic and industrial heritage. Ybor City dates back to the 1880s, when Cubans fled government oppression and came to the area to build cigar factories and homes for workers. Many Italian immigrants also settled in the area.

Tampa and its Ybor City prospered as dozens of factories produced hand-rolled cigars for which Tampa became well known. Mutual-aid societies in the Ybor neighborhood built ornate clubhouses and helped care for the health and welfare of their members. Each society's clubhouse served a particular ethnic group, such as the El Circulo Cubano for Cubans and the L'Unione Italiana for Italians. Club members gathered for a variety of social events from grand balls to political meetings to concerts or operas presented in a beautiful theater.

Like many other businesses, the cigar industry fell on hard times during the Depression. In addition, machines could produce cigars much more efficiently than hand rolling. Workers left Tampa to find jobs in New York factories. Ybor City began to deteriorate.

The neighborhood continued to decline through the next three decades. But in 1972 a Tampa publisher, Harris Mullen, bought several abandoned cigar factories and began to restore them. Today, Ybor Square, as the renovated buildings are called, is a delightful shopping and restaurant complex complete with an open courtyard for festivals and similar activities. Other business people and preservationists have followed Mullen's lead and have restored residential as well as commercial property. Civic leaders in Tampa believe the Ybor City neighborhood, with its historic buildings and ethnic character, will draw tourists and boost the city's overall economy.

In spite of the obvious benefits from such neighborhood preservation, restoration projects can sometimes displace longtime property owners. When property values go up, older residents may not be able to afford the increased taxes. Some may be forced to leave apartment buildings that are taken over by new owners who want to create condominiums, selling the apartments as high-priced single-family homes.

Robert Cassidy, in his book, *Livable Cities*, which covers grass-roots efforts to rebuild urban America, points out that "the displacement of current residents [in a neighborhood] can be avoided if the community organization establishes a clear set of goals and principles to that effect *before* the program gets started." Cassidy believes that human networks have to be preserved along with historical buildings.

THE GOVERNING NETWORK IN CITIES

CHAPTER NINE

Local government is "the most important level of government because it's closest to the people," says Mayor Johnny Ford of Tuskegee, Alabama, president of the National Council of Black Mayors. Commenting on gains made by blacks in recent mayoral elections, Ford told the editors of *Black Enterprise* magazine that he is well aware that new mayors, especially in big cities, have inherited many problems, from decaying infrastructures to high unemployment. But blacks are not winning elections simply because whites do not want to deal with urban problems. "There's still power in city hall," Ford declares.

Some of that power stems from the kind of influence a mayor has just by virtue of the office. Personal leadership also plays a part. Often a mayor can help determine who will get municipal jobs or contracts to do business with the city. Mayors who develop the art of negotiation and the ability to "sell" the benefits of their cities are sometimes able to bring new businesses to the urban area or to convince large corporations to invest in downtown renewal efforts. Helping to revive or improve the economy of a city can add to a mayor's prestige. Thus he or she gains more clout, or influence. Power seems to feed on itself, growing with use.

DIFFERENCES IN AUTHORITY

Mayoral power, however, sometimes depends on the system of government in a city. Some local governments have adopted a "strong mayor" system in which the mayor has extensive legal authority. Under such a system the mayor can appoint some city officials, develop a city budget, and propose local ordinances. But a city council, made up of elected representatives from different districts in a city, has the power to reject a mayor's appointments or budget. Only the council can enact proposed laws, although a mayor can veto measures passed by the council.

In this mayor-council form of government, as it is called, the mayor is the chief executive, the person responsible for seeing to it that everyday affairs of a city are handled smoothly and that the network of services functions effectively. The council is the lawmaking body (similar to a state legislature or the United States Congress), which writes up local laws and resolutions and helps maintain order in the city. The number of members on a council varies from state to state and city to city. In Indiana most cities have from seven to nine members on a city council. But in other states aldermen—one elected from each ward or district in a city—make up the council, which can include as many as fifty members.

The power of a mayor is quite restricted in cities with a council-manager form of government, or "weak mayor" system. In several thousand cities with this form of government, voters elect the mayor and council members and the council hires a manager as the chief executive who oversees the business affairs of the city. In some council-manager governments, the council chooses one of its members to serve as mayor. But the mayor simply represents the city at public ceremonies and conducts council meetings. As a council member the mayor can also vote on ordinances or on budget matters. Yet the mayor has no more authority than other councilors except in emergency situations such as an earthquake or a riot. When there is danger to the public, the mayor may take command of the police to keep order.

A city manager, on the other hand, carries out most of the executive duties ranging from preparation of the city budget to the selection of city employees for department heads. A city manager might also oversee most public works projects, although assistants are usually responsible for the day-to-day operations of city systems.

Because a city manager is chosen by a council and not by a public election, some critics of this form of local government say it is undemocratic. But in effect the manager does serve with the consent of voters, since he or she has been selected by the majority of the council, representing the people. The council also has the power to dismiss a manager who is not competent or works against the public welfare.

Proponents of the council-manager form of government believe it is the most "professional" way to govern. Usually, only people trained or educated in management are hired for city management positions. In fact, the council-manager government was modeled on the corporate structure, in which a board of directors decides company policy but hired managers or executives make the daily decisions required to run the firm. A city manager is supposed to be free of political influence and tend strictly to the business of the city. In practice, however, city managers often seek political support for programs or practices to be carried out by city governments.

"METROGOV" OR "UNIGOV"

In some parts of the nation, metropolitan-area governments have formed to meet the needs of rapidly expanding urban centers. As mentioned in the first chapter, the total count of SMSAs is over 300. One SMSA developed around Miami, Florida, during the 1950s. People moved out of the city or came to the suburban areas, settling in the small towns or in the unincorporated countryside of Dade County.

The county government could not provide all of the public services needed, and Miami was not able to extend city services outside its boundaries. After much study and many changes in city and county laws, the City of Miami and Dade County brought their governments together in 1957 to form the first metropolitan-area government. Voters elected a board of commissioners, who hired a county manager. The manager runs the metropolitan-area government just as managers run cities.

The Dade County government has sometimes been called a *federated* or two-tier form of government, a common structure in the metropolitan areas of Canada. With this form of government, the county oversees regional services such as public health and mass transit. But the city government and various boards and special-purpose districts provide local services such as police, fire protection, and schools.

Since 1970 Indianapolis, Indiana, has operated under a similar form of government called "Unigov," short for Unified Government. The boundaries of Indianapolis were extended to include the surrounding Marion County area. A nine-member city council and a five-member county council joined and expanded to become a twenty-nine-member city-county council, representing the city and suburban districts that became part of the city.

When Unigov was formed, supporters believed it would eliminate waste and duplication of services. Basically the structure of Unigov revolves around six departments: administration, metropolitan development, public works, transportation, public safety, and parks and recreation. The director of each department is appointed by the mayor, who is chief executive officer of the county. The mayor also appoints two deputy mayors. All appointed officials must be approved by the county council. This executive branch then carries out the daily operation of the city-council government.

A number of larger cities in the nation have also combined city and county governments. Honolulu, San Francisco, and Denver are examples. But most big cities operate separately from county governments.

WITHIN A STATE SYSTEM

No matter how varied the forms of local government, all must provide basic services such as water and sewer systems, street construction, police and fire protection, parks, and other public facilities. That is their only reason for being. But no local government can operate without the consent of the state as outlined in a charter, a kind of rule book or list of regulations. A city in the United States can do only what its state legislature or courts allow.

In some states a city cannot even tear down a billboard unless it has permission from the state. Perhaps a city wants to build a new stadium, but the charter does not contain any rules regarding such structures. The city must apply to the state courts, where the decision will be made on whether the city will be allowed a stadium.

Some city charters have been amended by the state courts so many times that they have hundreds of pages of regulations for all city business. Other charters are very simple. In some states all cities of a certain size have the same type of regulations and form of government. Still other states grant "home rule" charters that allow city governments to decide many local matters for themselves.

Most large cities in the nation have home rule charters, but the state legislatures still determine many local actions. The state of New York, for example, decides whether the city of New York can raise local taxes or increase its police force.

Some states may require cities to submit their budgets to a state agency for review, and the state might oversee other city financial affairs such as pension funds for local employees.

OVERLAPPING GOVERNMENT NETWORKS

Although New York City has a strong-mayor form of government, the city also operates under a system similar to a city-county government. Five boroughs (or counties) make up New York City; each elects a borough president to be a representative on the city council. Additional representatives are also elected to serve on the forty-three-member council. The mayor appoints deputies who are responsible for operations, policies, and economic development, but unlike a council-manager form of government, the deputies do not have to be approved by the council.

The executive level is only one of the branches of New York City government. Some local services are operated by boards or commissions, regional authorities, or special-purpose districts, such as the Board of Education, the Housing Authority, and the Metropolitan

Transportation Authority. These agencies or corporations are managed by their own executives, yet they receive some local funds and provide services for city residents under the jurisdiction of the local government.

Overlapping governments are part of every urban system. Often special-purpose districts are set up to provide a single service (such as regional transportation). Usually the special-purpose districts provide the human services such as health and welfare programs, while the city government is responsible for public works that could include police and fire protection and trash collection.

Some special-purpose districts, such as school districts, are set up as separate units of government so that they will not be influenced by local politics. Yet voters expect their schools to provide the types of programs and curricula that reflect the needs and desires of the community, so political efforts can affect the way schools operate.

Local residents and businesses also have to pay property taxes to support schools. At the same time, the state government determines the length of the school year, what should be taught, how teachers should be certified, and other regulations. Such overlapping authority can have political effects. It also may cause problems with *accountability*. That is, people expect government officials to account to citizens, to be responsible for actions taken as part of their governmental functions.

When there are dozens of special districts, authorities, or boards, a citizen often has no idea who is responsible for particular problems or where to go for help when services break down. Many districts and boards are operated by appointed officials and voters cannot even elect new people to replace officials who may be unsatisfactory.

MAKING WAVES

Even in small cities, where public officials are usually known and it is possible to reach a local council member, accountability is not always easy to achieve. Recently, in Elkhart, Indiana, an industrial city of 41,000, tenants in a federally funded public housing complex complained about roaches and rats in their apartments. Although the Housing Authority staff claimed that exterminators had cleaned up the buildings, the complaints went on. Some tenants tried to get help by calling members of the local board responsible for overseeing the operations of the complex. Others contacted a public official who lived in the neighborhood, the county councilman for the district, Ben E. Barnes.

Councilman Barnes is the only black elected official in the county government, and most of the black tenants in the city housing complex felt the councilman would listen to their complaints and try to rectify them. However, as Councilman Barnes tried to explain, neither he nor the county government had any authority over the housing units.

"But I made a few phone calls to some of the Housing Authority staff and board members to see what could be done," Barnes said. Although he was told that the buildings had been exterminated, Barnes decided, at the invitation of tenants, to see for himself. After inspecting several apartments, the councilman was convinced the pests were a real problem so once again he contacted the Housing Authority staff.

Several days later the situation had not changed. "The only recourse was the press," Barnes said. He knew elected officials could get coverage and reporters would jump on the story.

The result? A front-page headline and report on the pest problem, some attempts to place blame, and finally an extermination job that rid the buildings of roaches and rats.

POWER PLAYS

Calling attention to a problem or an issue via the media is a common practice for urban groups trying to effect positive changes in a neighborhood or community. But numerous groups use other methods to influence local government policies and functions. Firefighters, for example, might band together through their union to demand collective bargaining between city employees and the administration. If such bargaining does not take place, firefighters might threaten a strike to achieve their goal.

"Money talks," as the saying goes, in many efforts to influence government. Sometimes money is used in corrupt ways to bribe or extort. Officials may be asked to accept a bribe in money or other rewards in exchange for supporting certain legislation or helping someone get special treatment. Chicago has long been known for extortion practices in its building inspections. As an example, city inspectors may ask for or accept offers of money to overlook electrical wiring that does not meet city codes, or to issue a license for a business that does not meet safety rules. Sometimes individuals or business groups make payoffs to City Council members who will vote to change a zoning law that might allow a business or industry in an area that previously had been zoned residential.

Examples of corruption can be numerous and they are not confined to big cities. But for the most part, studies show that illegal practices to influence local government usually involve contracts to do business with the city, zoning (or how land will be used), and law enforcement, such as bribing an officer to "fix" a traffic ticket.

In spite of such illegal activities, money is often used in legitimate ways to influence local government action. Advertising campaigns to convince voters they should support certain government programs are certainly legal, but very costly. People with special interest in the programs may contribute funds for promotion.

Money also pays for lobbying efforts. Perhaps a group wants to stop construction of a state highway through one area of a city. Paid lobbyists would gather facts about the issue, testify against the highway proposal at public hearings, and discuss the proposal directly with individual lawmakers.

It is well known that money is important in political campaigns. Many interest groups try to have an effect on government by supporting candidates who share their views. Business leaders might form a group to back a mayoral candidate who promises to revitalize downtown. Black leaders might support a candidate who spells out plans to provide jobs for minorities. Both groups would have to raise funds for their campaigns. And the successful candidate would, no doubt, be influenced to some extent by the interest group that provided financial backing.

Some political scientists believe that in any city a fixed group of people—usually corporation and business leaders—influences the way local government operates. Still other urban experts argue against any one power structure. They cite the many variables and different groups that have an effect on local government decisions.

Whatever the power play used to affect the government network in urban America, local government must still deal with its primary function—providing services to people in the city, whether residents or visitors, workers or students, old or young, rich or poor. Without the proper services, the people who make a city will vote with their feet. They will influence government decisions by moving away from a city with deteriorating services to a city that responds to the needs of the community.

LIVABLE CITIES

CHAPTER TEN

Buenos Aires, Rome, Paris, London, Vienna, Toronto, Tokyo, Stockholm, and New York are just a few of the cities that people around the world point to as their favorite places. In spite of all the stresses and strains on urban systems worldwide, many cities are considered livable—places where the quality of life appeals to millions of people.

In the United States, a number of cities are often named as desirable places to live. San Francisco has been described as "a symphony of excitement, beauty, grace, and motion." To many New Yorkers, living in that city is like "living in the world." The windy city of Chicago is favored for its blustery "big shoulders" image, and Los Angeles for its vitality "leaping up genie-like off its sunbaked streets."

Atlanta, Boston, Dallas, Denver, Minneapolis, and San Francisco head a list of cities that corporate executives prefer, according to John F. Johnson, a vice president with Lamalie Associates, Inc., an executive search and placement firm. Business leaders also named a number of cities where they would least like to relocate. These included New York, Toledo, Detroit, Buffalo, and other eastern and mid-western cities that have severe unemployment problems.

Houston and Miami are also included among the least desirable. Johnson believes executives shy away from the problems of fast growth in Houston and the high crime rate and the effects of immigration in Miami. "In addition, for both cities, the cost of living has risen, and the onetime lure of an inexpensive life-style is disappearing," he said, adding that Houston may appeal more to corporate executives as the city continues to "rise as an international business center and headquarters for energy and energy-related industries."

What about the prospects for Miami, Detroit, Toledo, Buffalo, and New York? Will business people change their perceptions of those cities? "Time will tell," Johnson said. "People thought Cleveland was pretty terrible a few years ago, but I for one think it's a great place to live, work, and raise a family. In fact, I saw a life-style survey recently which ranked Cleveland in the top twenty locations in the United States—only its weather was rated dismal. . . ."

As Johnson pointed out, Cleveland has made a remarkable comeback. In December 1978 Cleveland became the first major American city since the Depression to default on its loans. Bankrupt Cleveland was unable to borrow money for two years. Financial problems and deteriorating city services went from bad to worse. But Cleveland's citizens and political and business leaders managed to form a coalition to raise city taxes, cut spending (especially padded payrolls), balance the city budget, pay off debts, and improve services. By 1982 the National Municipal League could name Cleveland one of ten "All-American" cities.

COMPETITION FOR HONORS

Cleveland and many other cities across the nation from Eugene, Oregon, to Charleston, South Carolina, are eager to be honored with the All-American label. Cities also actively compete for the Most Livable award presented by the United States Conference of Mayors.

Rating cities for livability has been going on since 1975, when the world-renowned newspaper, the *Christian Science Monitor*, ran a series on the quality of life in cities. At that time, Seattle was awarded the number one spot, which was a tremendous boost for a city with high unemployment and a "drizzly" image due to frequent rains.

Seattle began to glow after receiving its award. People in all sections of the United States, in Canada, and in other parts of the world became aware of Seattle's redevelopment efforts, which include a new downtown mall, a revitalized waterfront, a renovated historical area, and continual beautification programs for the city's parks, hilltop overlooks, huge botanical garden, and even a lake within its boundaries.

Fort Wayne, Indiana, an industrial city of 172,000, received the top rating for livability in 1983. And Mayor Winfield Moses says the honor will go a long way to change Fort Wayne's negative image, which has come about because of a number of unfortunate events: the 1980 assassination attempt on Vernon Jordan, then president of the National Urban League; floods that swamped the city in 1982; loss of the International Harvester plant, which put thousands out of work; and the grisly murders of a Fort Wayne newspaper executive and members of his family. All of these stories were carried on the national news media, making it difficult for the city to call attention to its assets.

Yet the Most Livable City title and an All-American City award (also won in 1983) will help to some extent in the city's efforts to attract new business and industry— the bottom line of the competition for city awards. As the mayor realistically put it: "You can't sell a city like Fort Wayne without . . . some certification of our quality of life. . . ."

Besides the municipal organizations that select cities as good places to work and live, dozens of publications make their own surveys and lists. *Places Rated Almanac,* for example, recently gave Atlanta the top rating for livability. In 1983 *Black Enterprise* magazine explored the quality of life for blacks in ten American cities and also rated Atlanta as tops. It is a city that some have dubbed "the capital of the black world," since it provides so many good economic opportunities for blacks.

In mid-1980, the *Chicago Tribune* surveyed dozens of American cities to learn whether our major urban centers were indeed falling apart. The report described many of the problems that continue to plague cities today—the fear of crime, decrepit public housing, energy and transportation crunches, and segregated neighborhoods, to name some. In older midwestern and eastern cities, people viewed the urban neighborhood "as a mostly scarred and perhaps doomed species."

The *Tribune* report also pointed out that cities are "no pleasure domes" for the poor, ill-educated, unskilled, and segregated. But there was another side. While problems in big cities get prime coverage, many cities with populations over 100,000 attract little attention. Reporters found "that scores of . . . cities contain vast areas that are eminently livable and untouched by blight. The worst of urban America has blinded us to the still-dominant good," the *Tribune* report concluded.

WHAT MAKES A "LIVABLE" CITY?

For the corporate executives surveyed by Lamalie Associates, quality-of-life factors are of prime importance if a city is going to be regarded as livable. Crime levels have to be low, public services have to be adequate, and schools must have good ratings. Government cooperation with business is also important to corporate people who want "a challenging work environment." Cultural attractions were another major consideration.

Louisville, Kentucky, a factory city with many blue-collar workers, has long known that its cultural achievements contribute to the "good life." Citizens support a repertory theater, orchestra, opera, ballet, an art museum, and countless preservation projects, at the same time pledging allegiance to its basketball teams and a new downtown mall called the Galleria.

During the fall of 1983, the Kentucky Center for the Arts in downtown Louisville opened its doors. The grand expanse of glass that fronts the $33.5 million complex reflects "a bit of Louisville's past," with images of neighboring buildings that have been restored. At night the building is lit only from the inside, "making it a giant lantern on Main Street that signals the vibrancy of the arts" in the area, as one observer described it. The center is expected to draw hundreds of thousands of Kentuckians to the city, as well as many more tourists from other parts of the nation. The influx of people should help the economy of the area.

New cultural centers are "leading the way in urban renovation," according to a recent report from *Newsweek* magazine. A new "palace of culture," the High Museum, opened in downtown Atlanta in November

1983 and several million visitors have been lured to the city center. The same is true of Dallas, Texas, where the block-long Museum of Art attracts people to the downtown "art district." In addition businesses are being built up around both cultural complexes, real estate prices have risen sharply, and the cultural centers are expected to employ many thousands by the year 2000.

"Kidspace" is another important aspect to people who want to raise families in cities. Usually this means cities should have not just huge parks and open areas, but courtyards in apartment complexes where young children can play on their "home turf." Clean waterways, public pools, safe playgrounds, outdoor skating rinks, and similar facilities are also part of what makes a city livable for children—and their parents.

NEW TOWNS

As older cities rebuild and revitalize their centers to improve the quality of life, some urban planners would like to see more emphasis on new towns. These are planned communities that are built by governments or by private companies to ease congestion in major urban centers and to provide housing and jobs for an increasing population. A variety of new towns have been built in England, Japan, Sweden, Israel, France, Poland, Russia, Canada, the United States, and many other countries.

The new town concept originated in Europe and many of these planned communities are based on Ebenezer Howard's ideas for a "Garden City" in Britain. Published in the late 1890s, Howard's master plan brought about a new industrial city that had most of the advantages and services one could expect to find in London at that time, plus "the beauties of nature," which could be enjoyed by all residents. Each metropolitan area was designed with green space surrounding it, keeping it separated and more unified, while at the same time providing countryside for city dwellers. In addition Howard proposed that urban areas surround a major core city in patterns similar to satellites around the earth.

England has led the way in the construction of new towns, under the British New-Towns Act of 1946. In the United States, "new towns" are as old as the nation in the sense that many cities were pre-planned. But there is no public policy or public development corporation to initiate planned cities as there is in England. Most Americans believe that private enterprise should be responsible for urban development, not the federal government.

During the 1800s, some new company towns were built as residential communities for workers. The Pullman Car Company, manufacturer of railroad sleeping cars, built the town of Pullman near Chicago in 1881. Other new towns were developed near major cities to serve large industries such as steel mills and automobile manufacturers. In the 1960s some new towns began with public funds used to acquire land for private development. Reston, Virginia, and Columbia, Maryland, are two examples. The construction of these well-planned communities has been privately financed, and both cities are geared to people with rising incomes and expanding leisure time. Thus, such new towns hardly address the problems of low-income urban dwellers who need jobs, housing, and other public services.

Through the Urban Growth and Community Development Act of 1970, federal funds were provided for a "New Towns Intown" program. Developers could borrow up to $50 million, with loans guaranteed by the federal government, to redevelop major cities on "a human scale." Little progress has been made, however, because of the rising costs of building and the high interest rates for loans. Urban development programs also suffer from a lack of comprehensive planning. Some city designers believe new towns should be "public ventures of a high order" as they are in Europe, where tax money is used for land and public facilities needed to establish urban areas.

FUTURE CITIES

A variety of experts predict a grim future for cities unless a national urban policy is forthcoming. But others foresee an urban renaissance, "a general reclamation of urban acreage," as Mayor Tom Bradley of Los Angeles put it. Author Isaac Asimov believes future cities will not be as important as they have been because new forms of communication will bring about increased decentralization. Cities, Asimov projects, may spread out "in orbit about the Earth. . . ."

Other projections for the future include domed cities in which the climate can be controlled, cities that float on oceans, and colonies on the moon. A gigantic "hexahedron" for 170,000 people was proposed in the late 1960s by Paolo Soleri. A model of the structure looks like two pyramids, one superimposed upon the other, designed for high-density living. Cesar Pelli's "megastructure" is another idea for a future city—in effect one continuous building where people could live, work, and enjoy recreational activities.

The plans, the models, the predictions, the vast amount of analysis on the future of cities can boggle the mind. No doubt, cities of the next century will still have some of the features of today's urban centers. Some will preserve historic buildings; others will incorporate new designs and technology. Whatever the visions, the cities of the future will have to be places where people can live and work, finding satisfaction and fulfillment in what they do.

INDEX